Puzzles for Young Children: Preparing Little Ones For Gifted
and Talented Tests & Private School Admissions
By Michael Wallach and El Otmani Ali
Published by Central Park Tutors Books
244 Fifth Avenue, Suite 2231, New York NY 10001
www.centralparktutors.com

Cover by El Otmani Ali
ISBN: 9780998834009
Printed in Canada

Table of contents

Introduction

The Puzzles

An Overview

We hope we can inspire you and your child with the puzzles in this book.

Today nearly all American children at the age of 4, 5 or 6 must take an intelligence test of some sort — whether to place into a gifted program or a magnet school, a private school, a charter school, or within their school to determine their academic track. The results of this test can have a profound impact on the resources and style of their future education for many years to come.

The good news is that you as a parent or teacher can help your child learn the skills to succeed at these tests. The even better news is that most children already have the intelligence to ace even the tests for "giftedness" and the most demanding of private schools. The best news of all is that learning the art of intelligence tests can be a joyous, playful process that builds on the natural curiosity and brilliance of all children.

Many years ago, our small New York City tutoring company was asked to help prepare little ones for these tests. We found quickly that there was a dearth of material that could be easily used by parents to prepare their children — and yet how were children supposed to learn this material if there was no simple way to practice it?

We had great success preparing our little ones, but we had to piece together material from a host of sources. The materials we found were disorganized and often cheaply put together — and what fun is a puzzle without color and beauty?

This is the book of puzzles we created to help children learn what admission and placement tests ask of them. We also took time to share as much as we could about how to work with your children in a joyous way that builds on their natural gift for learning.

In the pages that follow, we dig below the surface to look at the various forms of reasoning kindergarten entrance tests require. Then we offer some guidance for parents as to how to help children use their natural gift for learning to solve these reasoning puzzles. The second half of the book is a compendium of these puzzles, organized by the types of reasoning included in the most common admissions tests, with a short introduction to help you as a parent understand what is being tested.

Ninety puzzles are included in this book, each designed on a single page to allow you and your child to observe and consider the puzzle at length. Directly across from each puzzle are hints so that you have immediate access to guidance that can help your child learn the thinking techniques that will make him or her independent puzzle solvers.

Ultimately, we encourage you to see the puzzles in this book not as exercises to be broken down and taught but as puzzles to play with, and we encourage you to play this book of puzzles together with your child, just as you might sit down with him or her to play a game or read a story.

Indeed, we hope this book is as beautiful as your child's favorite illustrated story. Thanks to the incredible work of Moroccan artist El Otmani Ali, the pictures are based on the styles of more than fifty of the greatest artists of the twentieth century, from Picasso to Klee, Mondrian to Matisse, and so many more. Each puzzle has been designed to explore not only a form of reasoning that kindergarten tests attempt to measure, but a form of art and color, texture and composition, so as to inspire and speak to children's innate desire for beauty. Who more deserves to operate in a world of beauty than our children? Perhaps few appreciate it as much as they do.

We hope these puzzles help inspire your child to learn the skills of intelligence testing, and we hope you have a beautiful time working through these puzzles together with your child.

What Kindergarten Admissions Tests Measure

Most kindergarten tests, including most private school admissions tests, gifted and talented program entrance tests, and school ability tracking tests, are drawn from a series of intelligence tests developed largely over the last fifty years. The main underlying intelligence tests used are the Otis Lennon School Abilities Test, The Naglieri Non-Verbal Ability Test, the Wechsler Intelligence Scale, the Bracken School Readiness Assessment, and the Stanford-Binet Intelligence Scales. They each break down the concept of intelligence into various forms of reasoning — which they measure piece by piece.

Gifted and talented tests, private school admissions tests and tracking tests pull questions from these much longer intelligence tests to assess students. For instance, the New York City Gifted and Talented Test pulls half its material from the Otis Lennon School Abilities Test and the other half from the Naglieri Non-Verbal Ability Test. Many tracking tests pull material from the Wechsler Scale and the Bracken Assessment. Often, private school admissions tests pull material from a host of these.

Of the many skills assessed by these underlying intelligence tests (some are hundreds of questions long) there are ten forms of reasoning that reappear on numerous tests, and upon which the most popular kindergarten school entrance exams base their results. Each is included in this book. These are: 1. Pictorial and Figural Reasoning, 2. Pattern Recognition, 3. Reasoning by Analogy, 4. Sequential Thinking, 5. Spatial Visualization, 6. Aural Comprehension, 7. Aural Reasoning, 8. Quantitative Reasoning, 9. Letter Recognition and Phonemic Awareness, and 10. Number Recognition and Geometric Fluency.

The puzzles in this book are organized by type of reasoning. A short explanation of each type is included before the puzzles begin, so that you can understand what reasoning the tests measure yourself — and so that you can find a whole host of ways beyond this book to practice the thinking with your child. Many puzzles are the very same type of games that populate kids' favorite activity books; other puzzles are different, but can be equally fun challenges for kids.

To inspire you and your child, we have gone to great lengths to make our puzzles more beautiful than the ordinary intelligence test puzzle; however, since so much of success on entrance tests comes from learning how to apply intelligence to paper-based puzzles, we have mimicked as closely as possible the exact ways that questions are asked on entrance tests.

The reasoning types we selected directly mirror the NYC Gifted and Talented Test (the most widely administered Gifted and Talented Test) and the Kindergarten Readiness Test (the most widely administered Private School admissions test). Parents preparing their little ones for these tests will do well to simply work through the material in this book and practice each of the puzzles.

If your child is taking a different kindergarten admissions test, the material will most likely be quite similar. However, the wisest thing to do is to call the school or school system your child will be applying to and to find out exactly which forms of reasoning will be on the test — or at the least which underlying intelligence tests they are based on. If there are questions or forms of reasoning they will be asked that are not in this book, you can go to our website *www.centralparktutors.com/ puzzlesforchildren* to find extra material or suggestions of other books that might be helpful.

Whether or not the test your child ultimately takes mirrors the puzzles in this book, test scores in each of these ten skill areas have been linked to academic success later in students' lives. Put another way, learning how to translate innate reasoning ability to these kinds of tests does appear to undergird success in schools— even in areas that are not directly measured by the questions.

For instance, high scores in sequential reasoning skills help predict high mathematical test scores later in life. As childhood expert, and psychologist, Dr. Mel Levine explains: "Math is full of sequences. Almost everything that a child does in math involves following a sequence. Sequencing ability allows children to put things, do things, or keep things in the right order. When solving math problems, children usually are expected to do the right steps in a specific order to achieve the correct answer."

Similarly, noted Education Professor Usha Goswami has shown that children with strong reasoning by analogy test scores have higher reading scores earlier in life than those without them, because they can rely on those skills to learn new words and meanings.

In some areas, the classic forms of reasoning on the intelligence tests even surpass the latest trends in schooling. For instance, the Common Core entirely leaves out the development of pattern recognition in its current curricula for elementary schools. However, research which came out after the Common Core has shown that high pattern-recognition test scores significantly correlate with the ability of a student to score highly on math tests. By exploring pattern recognition questions with your children, you can thus help them not only do well on kindergarten tests, but help them build a foundation for mathematical learning that may be entirely skipped in their school but appear on other tests down the road.

Without a doubt, the tests measure important skills, and yet in our experience helping students prepare for these assessments, we have not found that the tests actually reveal students' potential. In many ways, the tests simply measure how well students are able to translate their innate reasoning skills onto a test. **In fact, in our experience, nearly all children possess the thinking skills to solve each of these types of problems.** Simply because your child does not do well on these questions initially does not mean they cannot reason or do not have the underlying ability being tested. It simply and most likely means they have not yet learned how to translate their abilities to the test.

For instance, "pictorial reasoning" is a test of a child's ability to classify various pictured objects. It thus purports to test a student's ability to classify in general. Yet my own son Lucas is proof that the skill in the abstract is quite different than the skill as tested.

Lucas fell in love with trucks, as so many young boys do, when he was only 18 months old, before he could say many words at all. Soon, he picked up the word "big" that my wife and I must have been using when he stared excitedly at trucks. "What a big truck" or "what a big bulldozer" we must have said so many times. Before long, he had created his own class of objects called "bigs." These were various forms of trucks and buses.

Lucas had shown he had a strong ability to classify, as almost all children do, right from the start. However, at the age of 18 months, had we sat him down for the classification section of "pictorial reasoning" he would not have done very well. To reason on a test is quite different than to reason in life.

Most children have not seen this type of material before and are therefore at a huge disadvantage if they are being asked to solve it for the first time on their test day. We strongly recommend waiting as long as possible for your child to take an entrance test — as their abilities and interest in working through paper-based puzzles can grow enormously as their developmental processes unfold. As any parent knows, even a few months can see extraordinary changes in children's ability to express themselves or desire to explore a type of game or story.

Thankfully, by the age of four or five, most students do have the ability to sit down and consider test material. If they are given exposure to the material and the chance to become comfortable with it through play and practice, then they are likely to be able to use their innate problem solving and reasoning abilities to easily maneuver through the many types of puzzles without difficulty.

There are of course, certain pressures not to prepare your child for intelligence tests. For a long time, many testing companies pushed the idea that intelligence is innate and test scores could not be improved with practice. We believe this is absurd. Of course students can improve their test scores by learning the material on tests. That's why teachers use tests in school! And with time, we have seen how even the biggest testing companies have altered their stance — from telling parents not to prepare, to selling the prep material themselves!

Whether or not to prepare your child for these tests is a very personal decision. Childhood is a fleeting world of beauty, and even at our tutoring company here in the heart of the competitive world of NYC education, we find ourselves cringing at the increasing pressures that children are more and more frequently put under. Nevertheless, many of us cannot escape the fact that our children will be tested, or will have to be tested if we are to offer them the best educational opportunities. So, we have taken a long look here at how to work with your children in ways that they will enjoy, in ways that allow them to apply their natural learning strategies to the puzzles on these tests.

This brings us to the foundational ideas of education — how children learn.

The Ingenious Ways That Children Learn

If the idea of preparing students for intelligence tests sounds daunting, it's worth remembering that by the age of three or four, the vast majority of children have already surmounted far greater feats of observation and analysis, involving the very types of reasoning on intelligence tests, and have done so with material far more complex.

The truth of the matter is that children are incredible learners. Any four-year-old who has learned how to speak — putting together basic grammar and vocabulary from the nearly infinite mass of data that confronts them over their first few years of life — has pieced together a puzzle that is so enormously complex it dwarfs the intelligence tests they may have to take and probably most other tasks they will be presented with later in life. In the words of lifelong educator and writer John Holt:

"We are so used to talking that we forget that it takes a very subtle coordination of lips, tongue teeth, palate, jaws, cheeks, voice and breath. Simply as a muscular skill it is by far the most complicated and difficult that most of us ever learn. How does the child do it? The answer seems to be by patient and persistent experiment; by trying many thousands of times to make sounds, syllables, and words; by comparing his own sounds to the sounds made by people around him; and by gradually bringing his own sounds closer to the others; above all, by being willing to do things wrong even while trying his best to do them right."

This way of thinking — the combination of observation, play, and patient, persistent experimentation — is at the heart of the child's natural and ingenious learning process. Through following this process, we believe that most children can learn the puzzles that claim to separate the "gifted and talented" or the "highest track" from others.

Author and TED speaker Ted Wujek performed an insightful and amusing series of experiments to demonstrate the power of this type of thinking. He asked numerous teams from different sectors of society to construct the tallest structure they could with a handful of dried spaghetti, scotch tape, and a marshmallow. The teams had a limited amount of time, and the structure had to have the marshmallow at the top.

Of all the teams that participated, the worst performance of all came from the group of recent business school graduates. Among the very best, far outscoring the average, were the teams of kindergarteners (who scored second only to architects and engineers, thank goodness).

Why were the kindergarteners so much better at building these structures than the vast majority of adults? Wujec's research showed it was their process of actively experimenting, rather than analyzing and then building. While most adults attempted to get their heads around the problem first, and then build a structure, the kindergarteners were far more likely to dive into building the structure, seeing it fail, gaining insight from that, and then rebuilding a new structure with the new information. Most kindergarteners were able to thus build several experimental buildings in the time that it took adults to build only one (one which usually fell). In Wujec's words:

"What kindergarteners do differently is that they start with the marshmallow, and they build prototypes, successive prototypes, always keeping the marshmallow on top, so they have multiple times to fix when they build prototypes along the way. Designers recognize this type of collaboration as the essence of the iterative process. And with each version, kids get instant feedback about what works and what doesn't work."

John Holt, educator and cellist, speaks eloquently of it as well. On dozens of occasions throughout his teaching career, Holt would stop by a classroom with his cello.

"I have seen perhaps a 100 young children try out the cello... I always play if asked, and one of the pieces I play is the prelude to the first of the Bach cello suites... It is a very active piece — my right arm moves rapidly up and down as well as back and forth... When I then ask the children (and adults) if they want a turn, the children all start out by trying as far as they can to do just what I was doing. They are not so much trying to figure out how to play the cello as actually playing it... Do they think "I'm going to do just what John did" expecting to get the same results, or "I am going to do all the things he did and see what happens?" The younger ones may really think or hope at first that they can get the same results that I can. Perhaps not... young children show clearly when they are disappointed, and I have never seen a young child look disappointed by the results of what he was doing with the instrument...

In time, they realize they are not making quite the same kinds of sounds I made... and they grow tired of doing nonsense, and begin to want to try to figure out how the cello really works. But the total activity comes first.

It doesn't take a child long, by such steps, to grasp the basic idea of the cello, but while he has been figuring this out, he has been ceaselessly active. One could say that he is having too much fun — a weak word really— playing the cello to want to take time to figure it out... His way of attacking the problem is to produce the maximum amount of data possible, to do as many things as he can, to use his hands and the bow in as many ways as possible. Then as he goes along, he begins to notice irregularities and patterns. He begins to ask questions — that is to make deliberate experiments. But it is vital to note that until he has a great deal of the data, he has no idea what questions to ask or what questions there are to be asked... The young child, at least until he is spoiled by adults, has a great advantage... he is much better at taking in this data, to tolerate confusion, and he is much better at picking out patterns, hearing the faint signal above the noise, but the greatest difference between children and adults is that most of the children to whom I offer a turn on the cello accept it, while most adults... refuse."

Part of the inspiration to write this book came from the desire to create materials that we felt we might want to share with our son Lucas. One time, when he was quite young, he found a whole box of individual toy styrofoam letters at a friend's house. He immediately saw them as wonderful objects to put in a butterfly net. "Look Dad, letters!" he exclaimed in the delight of recognition, carrying out the letters to me. We put them on the ground and began to play. He wanted to know what a few of them were called, and then moved on to playing with them in different ways. The pile included numbers as well, and so I placed the number 8 on 8 stones, to signify it's meaning, but my son was not interested in this lesson. He saw something different — an opportunity to put each letter on "a chair of its own." Methodically, he went and gathered dozens of stones and placed each letter on its "chair."

Was Lucas learning what each of the letters sounded like? Was he learning what they "meant"? No, but he was observing them, he was learning their shape, their look, and occasionally he would ask their name. Ever after that, he would find those same letter shapes all around, in pretzels and bread, with popsicles sticks or on signs, and then shout out the names to me. He was learning the letters in his own way, a way filled with joy and play, and a way which will cement his understanding quite firmly over time, far more fluidly than had I set him down against his own desires to "learn" the letters in one swoop, or some repeated pattern of swoops. Children see in their own way — a joyous, ingenious way.

The natural learning process of children is a wondrous thing to consider and to behold, and we encourage you to use this book in accordance with this natural process. It is a process that begins with their choices, carrying through from the first act of picking up the book to the great challenges in not giving up on a puzzle that at first perhaps seems to them quite difficult.

If we can encourage you with any idea, it's simply not to worry about "teaching." We do not have to "teach" a child to develop his mind through thinking any more than we have to teach a child to develop his body through play. Children love to learn — not all day, not everything. But when they are surrounded with healthy play for the mind, they will dive in as eagerly as they do a slide at the playground.

Applying Children's Natural Learning Strategies To Intelligence Puzzles

It's easy to forget how much new information these puzzles present to a child's eye. The colors, shapes and patterns alone are enough to fire up a child's imagination, and the "answers" that the tests are looking for may be quite different than the thought processes that fire off when children first encounter the puzzles.

We encourage you to meet children where they are — both in their exploration of puzzles and in their attempts to solve them. Children's natural learning processes offer a great way to understand how to do this.

We have organized each section of challenges in this book to begin with puzzles that kids can relate to — trucks and flowers, animals and dinosaurs. These are also the easiest questions. Start with these relatable questions and work your way through each section to explore more and more abstract forms of thinking, working towards the often quite abstract kind of puzzle challenges that entrance tests require.

As students begin to work their way through the puzzles, their natural learning strategies will begin to reveal themselves.

When presented with the direct questions asked by the puzzles, often students will begin to guess, almost randomly. Rather than sit back and try to analyze the puzzle in their head, as adults did in the Wujek Marshmallow experiment, children love to push and tinker in any way they can to learn about the puzzle. Since they often don't know what to ask, or how to formulate their questions, many children ingeniously press on, by randomly guessing answers and seeing what information that provokes from the adult in the room.

For many children, the response to the initial puzzle question (e.g. what is missing in this puzzle) will thus be to guess randomly at answer choices. We encourage you not to see this as a sign of incompetence in "solving" puzzles, laziness or lack of effort. Guessing randomly is an active strategy for children, and when understood as such, can be an extremely helpful form of teaching interaction. Just as the children in Wujek's Marshmallow experiment generated information simply by building unsuccessful towers, when children guess at the answer to a puzzle they don't yet understand, they are generating information — your answer — from which to learn.

When they point to a puzzle answer that doesn't fit in the puzzle, it's helpful to consider that they are not so much saying, I think it's this one. They are examining: what will you say if I pick this one? What about that one? And your answer can be, if understood correctly, helpful to them in learning how to think and analyze the puzzles in the future. Thus the most helpful answer is not some version of "come on, try harder, or hey think about it," offering a commendation that that was a good guess alone, or some other purely motivational response. The most helpful answers give the child information about the puzzle and its answers.

Upon an "incorrect" guess, we might say, "well, that's a good start. That could go in the box, but it doesn't fit because the top corner is orange and in the painting the corner is blue. Can you find an answer that has the right color in the corner?" Now, the next time they guess, they may guess somewhat randomly again, but they will most likely guess an answer that solves the blue corner problem. Again, we might say, "That's a great second step, to guess that answer. That has the right color in the corner here, but it's missing the stripe over here on this side. Can you find the answer with the right color and the right stripe?" Now they will guess again, and they will likely get it right. The next time they come upon this question, they may guess again. Worry not! Does this mean they haven't "learned" what you thought they had learned last time? Not at all. It means they haven't yet committed to it, fully taken it into their confidence. As the educational philosopher David Hawkins writes, "All of us must cross the line between ignorance and insight many times before we truly understand." If your child guesses again on a problem they have seen before, simply repeat these steps. Repeat and repeat, always viewing "guesses" as attempts to draw helpful information from you. It is through this process of interrogating you via guesses that your child learns.

Children's natural process of observation and patient, persistent experimentation also, very crucially, involves play. Here is another story from Holt about this process.

"Bill Hull and some other friends of mine were developing a very ingenious and powerful set of mathematical and logical materials called A-blocks. They are a set of various wooden blocks of different colors and sizes. They developed these materials by having small groups of young children, mostly five year olds, work with them. They found it a very interesting thing about the way children reacted to these materials. If, when a child came in for the first time, they tried to get him "to work" right away, to play some of the games and solve some of the puzzles, they got nowhere. The child would try to do what he was asked to do, but without joy or insight. But if at first they let the child alone for a while, let him play with the materials in his own way, they got very different results. At first, the children would work the pieces of wood into a fantasy, construction, animals, houses and cars... When, through such play and fantasy the children had taken these materials into their minds, mentally swallowed and digested them, so to speak, they were then ready and willing to play very complicated games, that in the more organized and business-like situation had left other children completely baffled. This proved to be so consistently true that the experimenters made it a rule always to let children have a period of completely free play with the materials, before asking them to do directed work with them."

Often students interact in their own way with the puzzles at hand, and not in the way we have been trained to expect them to answer. Many children will see in the puzzles aspects interesting to them which are not "finding the answer." This may be to draw on the puzzle, to turn it upside down, or to point out interesting things about the puzzle. This is a great way for students to interact with and learn aspects of the puzzles. Most important, it is the expression of their natural curiosity and interest. Encouraging this is the most helpful way to "teach" students how to eventually answer the puzzles.

If a student sees the puzzle and points out the colors, encourage this, point to other colors in the painting, and see if together you can name them all. Perhaps point to the different shapes. Give funny names to funny shapes. The next time you see the puzzle with the student, you can interact in a new way. You can start by naming the colors again, or the objects, or the way the lines are drawn, and this time ask other questions. "Do you see the puzzle pieces at the bottom? Let's find the colors in those too. Which one has the same colors? Which looks like it might fit in the hole?" It's likely that this time, the child will be more likely to entertain your questions, once they have examined it in their own way. They might guess at the answers randomly at this point, but the interaction has changed. And now you can work through the guesses with them as we spoke about above.

A third way children learn is simply through conversation. Just as young speakers are unlikely to start a conversation, but may engage after a while, so too young puzzle solvers are likely to learn enormous amounts from simply observing and discussing.

In fact, many children may simply not understand how they are "supposed" to see a puzzle. They may wonder how one is supposed to look at these puzzles. Rather than jumping to some elaborate explanation about how to "do" the puzzle, simply observe and converse about it. You can point out the background and foreground colors, or the aspects of the puzzle that strike you. By simply observing the pictures yourself, and verbalizing what aspects of the pictures strike you, you can help your child to think along the same lines. Not only does this help engage a child in the puzzle at hand, they are also learning the concepts of observation — background and foreground, shapes and contours, color palettes and patterns — that make up the substance of puzzle observation.

Often, children scan a work of art for something to connect to, much as we do as adults in a museum. They simply may not find anything to connect to in the puzzle at hand, and thus might lose interest. That's okay! We have designed these puzzles to include objects of interest to young children, but not all of the puzzles include these objects because many questions in kindergarten testing do not have these. If a student is not interested in a puzzle, skip it. Turn the page to find another puzzle that has an object of interest for them — perhaps a truck, a cookie or a flower. Take a look at this puzzle with them, and interact with them in this way. Perhaps allow your child to scan through the book to find objects they appreciate. Most likely, there will be puzzles with objects that interest them. By working through the puzzles with objects that interest them, the fun of puzzle solving is likely to infect them, and you can move on to work through other puzzles with this idea in mind...

After a while, you may find that you are going over some, or all, of the puzzles again, rather than moving on to "tougher puzzles." That too is okay. One of the wonders of children is their joy in repeating activities they enjoyed in the past. Kids love to read the same stories over and over again, to draw the same picture a hundred times, to play games in the very same spot they played them the time before. As master logicians, it actually makes enormous sense. Children are used to encountering a million aspects of the world around them that may or may not be hard and fast rules. A door opens, and a child's mommy is behind it. The child opens the door again — will there always be a mommy behind it? Children quickly learn to be natural skeptics, testing and retesting theories to see if they continue to hold true. Through solving the same puzzles in the same way over and over again, children learn to concretize what they have learned.

Simply because your child may have worked through all of the puzzles successfully doesn't mean he or she will not gain insight (and joy) from completing the puzzles again. We encourage you to go through the book with your child multiple times if your child is interested in doing so, rather than trying to quickly move on to "new" material. Puzzles and images are quite complex, and children are naturals at "scaffolding" their own learning — examining and re-examining the same things and gaining new information from them each time. Perhaps your child wants to show you how well she knows the answers, or perhaps she is not sure and wants to challenge herself again. Right answers are just as good an opportunity for concretizing into their mental map the ideas in the puzzles as wrong answers are in learning it. If your child selects the right answer to a puzzle, have a conversation with him about how he got there. This can be as simple as remarking "Yes, that's right, that fits because the colors match and the shapes match," or it can be a longer conversation "How did you figure that out?" Your children may not respond right away, as meta-cognition is often not as easy for children to speak about as reflex memory, but a few remarks about why they are right can help reinforce the strategies they develop and their confidence in approaching puzzles in the future.

Sometimes a child has difficulty solving a puzzle and wants to continue with it, using other methods. Below are two test-taking strategies that are also ways to think through puzzles more deeply and help students back into the loop of play, observation, conversation, and experimentation that children naturally use.

These methods include **drawing** (either actually or in an imaginary way) information as necessary and **imagining** each answer as a potential answer and then evaluating it. In fact, these strategies are quite helpful to the thinking process itself.

By **drawing** in information that they would like, kids can make visible the information that was previously only audible or, even simply in their head, concrete. For instance, students might benefit in their thinking by drawing down vocalized instructions in the "following directions" section of the test, or they might benefit by drawing in the quantitative section. If a child is told that each nest holds three birds and asked how many birds there would be if she has two nests, she may be initially overwhelmed by the amount of information. By taking the time to draw three birds next to each nest, and then counting up the birds, she can break down the information into sizable and useful pieces, becoming actively involved in figuring out the problem and using her imagination, and then using all of this to arrive at the solution. This is the very best of what can be meant by test-strategies and we highly recommend it.

Imagining each answer as "the" answer is another helpful method for children to think more deeply through a puzzle. This can be done either in their imagination, by drawing in each answer, or even by cutting out various answer choices with scissors and seeing which one fits. When teaching this strategy, go ahead and cut up the book! Or if you prefer, make a copy of a puzzle and its answers and then cut this one up. The visual and tactile additions of being able to actually move the puzzle piece is extraordinarily helpful in the learning process. After a few times of cutting up a puzzle, kids should be able to "cut it up" in their head and move it into the box. Seeing each answer in the missing box of a puzzle can then become a way of discussing the puzzle in more depth. We highly encourage you to do this with your child when they make an incorrect guess. Imagine that guess as the answer (or cut it out and place it in there!) and then have a discussion about it. What works about that answer? What doesn't work? This is a fantastic and basic way to discuss the puzzle in detail.

But that only leads us back to what we hope to stress again and again: nothing is more important than simply the act of observation, and these strategies are, at heart, aides to the process of observation. More fundamentally, the best aide of all is simply to engage in conversation about the puzzles with your children. Follow their lead, let them talk about the puzzles in their way, and you in yours. As practiced searchers of hidden rules, expert observers of the world and eager, curious insatiable thinkers, they are likely to bring insight and joy to the task which can lead them through it. We can think of no better guides to this process beyond the love of a caring parent or teacher.

Persisting Through Difficulty

Of course, at times your child may show total and complete lack of interest. If your child is not at all interested in the puzzle book, it doesn't mean he or she will be uninterested forever. It's important to respect that lack of interest, otherwise you may find yourself in a battle of wills, and as any parent knows, the will of a four year old is a mighty force. Worse, if the puzzle book is forced upon them, a child may come to view the book as something he or she doesn't like as a matter of independence.

Rather than trying to force or cajole a child into liking the book, we recommend putting it away for a while. Perhaps at this point in their development, these children need other forms of play and exploration. Perhaps they need physical activity or more story-based restful activity. By putting the book away and coming back to it, a week or a month later, you may find a very different response altogether. Holt speaks of many students who, when they encounter difficulty, simply need a break.

"How much people can learn at any moment depends on how they feel at that moment about the task at hand. When we feel powerful and competent, we leap at difficult tasks... At other times, we can only think, "I'll never get this, it's too hard for me." Part of the art of teaching is being able to sense which of the moods these learners are in. People can go from one mood to another quite quickly. In Never Too Late, I wrote about an eight-year-old who could go from an up mood to a down and then back up, all in a thirty-minute cello lesson. When people are down, it's useless to push them or urge them on; that just frightens and discourages them more. What we have to do is draw back, take off the pressure, reassure them, console them, give them time to regain — as in time they will — enough energy and courage to go back to the task."

As a way to inspire your child, you may also consider taking the book yourself and studying it sometime without forcing it upon them. Allow your child to see you experiencing the book. Indeed, each puzzle has been inspired by a great work of art in the twentieth century. Across from each puzzle is a reference of the painting and the painter who inspired each illustration. Can you figure out who the artists are or were? Find the paintings online. Do you see the similarities? If, during this time, you haven't already found your child creeping up to discover what you are doing with this book, and it is hard to imagine you won't, keep investigating. Imagine each of the painters painting your house. Which would you prefer? Cut out some puzzles and put them on objects in your house you think they would look pretty upon. Don't hold the book as a sacred object which cannot be explored in your own way. Explore it! Have fun with it. There is nothing more infectious to a child than a parent or teacher playing with their toys creatively.

It is hard to imagine that at some point they won't want to participate, even by asking questions. And this is the beginning of the investigatory journey.

Despite all of the attempts you may make to ensure that your child's journey through this material is joyful and play-based, you may still encounter moments when your child feels frustrated and discouraged by the complexity of the puzzles. Again, we write with strong encouragement to remind you and your child that this is a natural part of the learning process. How we respond when our children face difficulty can have a huge impact not only on how they fare on the test, but how they choose to overcome difficulties in the future.

We run a small tutoring company in NYC, and we have had numerous students now score in the very top percentiles of the test and earn entrance to the city's Gifted and Talented schools and programs, even though they were scoring in the 50th percentile range when we began to work with them. We strongly believe that diagnostic tests and past performance should not be read as predictors of a child's future score, but as maps for how and where to build their curiosity, joy, and skills.

One of our teachers wrote to us a helpful story about working with two students to prepare for the 8th-grade Specialized High School Admissions Test. Each student came to her scoring in the mid 50th percentile on their diagnostics, and yet each student, after only about four months of tutoring, at only two to four hours a week, scored in the top 5th percentile of students in the whole city. By any normal scholastic measure, this is an extraordinary, startling level of growth. But experienced educators know that children are always capable of extraordinary growth, if they are listened to and helped through the particular barriers confronting them.

In this case, each of these students had very particular needs. One student had simply never seen a whole semester of mathematical concepts that were on the test. Faced with a test asking her to do things she had never done before, she froze. Once our tutor Emily discovered this, and discovered which concepts she had missed, they went over them together one by one. The student quickly learned them and went on to exceed the score to qualify for the most competitive school in the city.

The other student was quite different. He had already seen all the math on the test and fancied himself a strong mathematician. He was a straight A student in his math class at school and had been for years. Yet he had not seen the phrasing of questions as they were put on the test he was now facing. When he encountered the strange and puzzling wording, his self-esteem was suddenly challenged in an area he considered himself a pro. He found this very upsetting and would stop investigating the problems, even though if he could only get over this hump, he was a great mathematician.

Emily's response was to be consistently encouraging and to help him develop an inner dialogue he could have with himself as he worked through the problems — if frustrations came up, he knew what to say to himself. Rather than viewing the problems as something he had to know or not know the answer to, he retrained himself to view them as something to be tinkered with, explored, and discovered.

How children approach difficulty is a subject Carol Dweck, a Professor of Education at Stanford, has studied in depth. Her research unpacks the stories students tell themselves, and the stories we tell children, when they encounter difficulty. Her suggestion is to try to take the idea of "intelligence" out of the equation altogether.

Though it's become almost taken for granted by many to reassure children that they are "smart enough" to tackle a problem or task, Dweck warns against re-enforcing the idea of intelligence as a fall-back when students have a hard time. Dweck's research shows that children perform far better on long-term academic tasks when they are encouraged to see academic work as something that may be difficult but which needs to be tinkered with and played with, not something they are "smart enough" to do easily if they keep trying.

In other words, if a student feels that a puzzle is "hard," that's a good thing.

Dweck explains that students who view intelligence as fixed tend to turn away from problems that they cannot immediately solve, while those who see intelligence as something that grows from practice tend to welcome challenges as something that helps them grow. Because of that, these students are regularly able to surpass the academic achievements of their peers.

Dweck goes on to explore our own ideas of giftedness and genius. Think about Thomas Edison, she writes:

"He's in New Jersey. He's standing in a white coat in a lab-type room. He's leaning over a light bulb. Suddenly, it works! Is he alone? Yes. He's kind of a reclusive guy who likes to tinker on his own.

In truth, the record shows quite a different fellow, working in quite a different way… There are many myths about ability and achievement, especially about the lone, brilliant person suddenly producing amazing things… Yet Edison was not a loner. For the invention of the light bulb, he had 30 assistants, including well-trained scientists, often working around the clock in a corporate funded state-of-the-art laboratory!

It did not happen suddenly. The light bulb has become the symbol for that single moment when the brilliant solution strikes, but there was no single moment of invention. In fact, the light bulb was not one invention, but a whole network of time-consuming inventions each requiring one or more chemists, mathematicians, physicists, engineers, and glass blowers.

Yes, Edison was a genius. But he was not always one. His biographer, Paul Israel, sifting through all the available information, thinks he was more or less a regular boy of his time and place… What eventually set him apart was his mindset and drive."

Indeed, the vast majority of those who are named "gifted" and "talented" by gifted and talented tests turn out not to be any more gifted than the average child. True "giftedness" is so rare that many in the scientific world consider it a mirage... And studies have shown that possibly more than 80 percent of students who are categorized as "gifted" ultimately do not remain so on intelligence tests in later years. In fact, schools, through testing, have been shown to be significantly worse at determining "giftedness" than parents themselves, despite the obvious bias that a parent has towards their child. Perhaps this "bias" is more about the ability to see the beauty of their child's mind more easily than those who do not know the child as well.

Sometimes students are able to show enormous progress just when some thought they were never going to grow at all. So many students are asked to tackle tasks such as standardized tests and top-down directed school work that bears no interest for them that eventually they find that their natural curiosity and passion for learning has been destroyed, and their interest in the world wanes. Sometimes these children are seen as incapable of learning altogether.

My wife Susana, a former English teacher who had become a private tutor, had just such a student. He was in 9th grade, but reading on a 5th-grade level. He was described as totally uninterested in anything academic, and his parents wondered if he would ever graduate from high school at all. His administrators saw him as mischievous, suffering from emotional disorders and ADHD that led them to believe he lacked the focus necessary to learn the skills that would ever be needed to read. They asked my wife to work with him one on one, clearly relieved to be handing off a "problem child."

Susana began working with him not by breaking down his skill level and forcing him through the mountain of sheets that could have filled a room with his lack of skills. She got to know him. She tried to see the world through his eyes.

"When we first met, my student said to me right off the bat, "I don't like books, books are boring." I don't know why this time was different, but I challenged him. "It's impossible," I said. "To say books are boring means you think stories are boring. A human who doesn't enjoy stories is about as likely as a monkey who doesn't like to swing in trees. Humans are story. You haven't found what you like." The room fell quiet and we continued with our lesson on pronouns. I wracked my brain. I finally remembered another student, who was also a reluctant reader and about the same age, who'd become hooked on the Cirque du Freak series. Well, I knew that handing Joey the book and saying, "Give it a try. You'll love it" would be the equivalent of me trying to tackle Jean-Paul Sartre's autobiography in its original French: not happening. Like a candy salesman trying to hook her customer, I decided to let him taste the sweetness, in hopes of getting him so addicted that he would do anything to get more — even if that meant reading on his own.

I began reading aloud to him and he was immediately addicted. Each day when our time finished, he begged for more. Hearing fluent reading is beneficial for developing fluency and nuanced reading, major factors in comprehension, so I was excited he was spending so much time listening to me read aloud, but I was determined to have him fall in love with reading, and to actually read. Luckily I'd picked a twelve-book series, so when we finished the first book I agreed to delve into the second only if he read every fourth page.

I dreaded when it was his turn to read. He stumbled, I corrected, and we both felt bad. But after a couple of weeks I started noticing an improvement — nothing monumental but enough to keep my hopes up. I hated correcting him and trusted my instinct enough to do research on what literacy experts recommend.

I was relieved to learn studies show that correcting a child during read aloud is counterproductive, as it frustrates and embarrasses them to the point of avoiding it altogether, so I stopped. It was difficult to stay quiet when he butchered common words, but I knew if I wanted to hook him I had to let it go.

We read two 200+ page novels in three weeks. He begged for more and I agreed as long as he read every third page. We continued this way – I modeled, he butchered— for another two books. His progress was slow and I started worrying my plan was going to fail.

Then one day Joey came running into the classroom saying he couldn't take the suspense anymore and had finished the novel on his own. The boy who "hated books" had read 100 pages on his own in one night! I was stunned and delighted. When I had tested Joey at the beginning of the year, he was reading at a sixth-grade level. By the end of the year and twenty novels later (five of which he read independently), he was reading at a tenth-grade level. On the last day of school I proudly gave him a sterling silver bookmark with his name engraved on it."

We encourage you to believe in the incredible intellect that lives in all children. And when they encounter difficulty, we encourage you to listen to them and search to understand the emotional or academic underpinning of their difficulty. Sometimes students need to be taught a clear, and well-organized, skill-based lesson; sometimes they just need to be read a good book. Maybe your son or daughter wants to watch you solve the puzzles yourself. If that's what they want: go for it! You can always return to do the book with them again down the road.

A final word...

Many parents ask us how long to work with their children to prepare them for tests. Every child truly is different - some will breeze through certain sections and others will not; what trips up two children about a puzzle may be entirely different, the way they solve them may be different as well -so we are hesitant to put a number on how long to work with a child on this material.

However, to give you a rough sense of timing, we recommend spending at least 2 hours per section with your child if you are preparing them for an admissions test. More than likely, they will finish some sections more quickly than that, and will explore other sections for much longer. Giving them roughly two hours a week for three months prior to the test is roughly the amount of time we would spend directly preparing. However, if along the way you discover that your child truly needs extra time exploring a certain kind of reasoning, there is no need to be alarmed. Now you have a guide as to what to spend extra time learning about.

The puzzles in this book are laid out by form of reasoning, progressing from simplest to most complex, and before each type we have listed a short explanation of the reasoning the tests are looking for, along with some thoughts on how to expand your child's puzzle-thinking beyond the contours of this book.

We hope these puzzles give you and your child a strong sense of what intelligence tests are measuring and how to help your child learn these skills. They are certainly not the only way of learning them. There are other books of exercises, and there are a myriad of wonderful games — from jigsaw puzzles to building blocks, simple painting and drawing to books of other types of word games, legos and games with paper mâche. Many children's activity books are rife with games that mimic the intelligence tests. The list of games is so long and varied that it is silly to attempt to make one here. One of our intentions with this book is simply to reveal to you as a parent or teacher the underlying material of the tests, so that if you see the material presented in another way in the toy store, book store, or in your daily life you can immediately recognize it as something helpful for your child.

Of course, the very best way for students to develop their intelligence in the long run is to let them do all the things that children love — to read books with you, to play games, to build castles, to draw pictures, to play music and to have interesting conversations. We cannot stress enough that it is through self-directed creative play and conversation that children truly learn and grow in their reasoning skills, skills which will ultimately translate to the reading, math, and thinking skills that schools require. Nothing is more important than simply spending time with your child and listening to them, speaking with them, reading with them, and playing with them.

However, we hope that with the puzzles in this book you can help them learn to apply those skills on the tests they will face as they enter kindergarten. Most of all, we hope through this book that you and your child enjoy the time spent learning these skills together.

Mike Wallach Founder
Central Park Tutors

The puzzles

Pictorial and Figural Reasoning

Pictorial and Figural Reasoning. These questions ask children to see a picture or series of pictures and be able to think critically about how to classify them. This involves recognizing the objects, and then, on a second level, associating them with various different classes of objects. Sounds complicated? It's not.

For example, a set of objects may all be one color, except for one. Or a set of objects may all be trucks, except for one. More complex questions ask students to recognize more complex classes — such as mammals, tools, or drinks. These questions also ask students to find abstract classes that require careful study — such as which objects all show the same color pattern or the same number of corners. Speaking through your own study of the objects and vocalizing your thought process is a great way to show children that they can do this too, and that the search for the answer is a journey, not an immediate discovery.

Typically, these questions ask students either to pick out the object which does not "fit" with the others or they ask students to positively point out classes of objects. For instance, a student might be asked to circle all of the vehicles in a picture, or to find all of the things that live in the forest.

To build these test skills outside of the book, you can take steps as simple as asking for objects in your house through this type of language — instead of asking for a banana, you can ask for a yellow fruit, and let them search through items for it; or instead of milk, ask them to bring you something you can drink, which is white.

Another simple game is to turn this around and see what you can come up with for classes that an object can fit it. Start by explaining the idea of the game — we're going to talk about all the things a banana is. It's a fruit; it's a food; it's a yellow thing; it's something monkey's eat; it's a curved thing, etc. After playing this game two or three times, your child is likely to play it with you with all sorts of various objects, and the many ways of classification will come to the fore.

Inspiration :

Toru Fukuda - Doodles

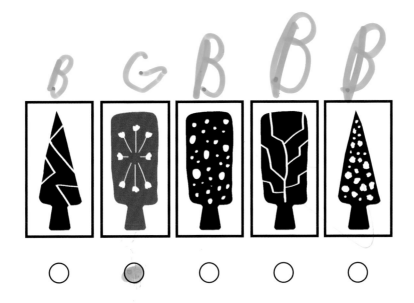

Which of these pictures does not belong with the others?

Hints :
Which picture is of a different animal than the others?

Inspiration :
Jacques Rouxel - Les shadocks

Answers :
First box on the left

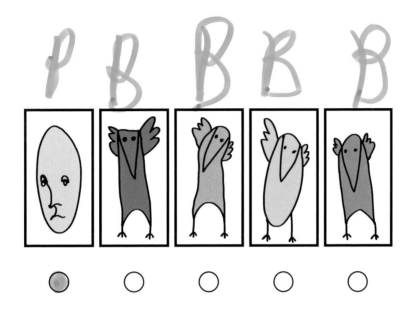

Which of these pictures does not belong with the others?

Hints :
Which one is not a car?

Inspiration :
Unknown artist - Inside the rainbow

Which of these pictures does not belong with the others?

Hints :

What is the same about all of the pictures except one? What is different about that one?

When you are trying to figure out what doesn't belong, you can look at shape, color, size, background, and anything else that you see.

Inspiration :
Yayoi Kusama - Artist style

Answers :
First box on the left

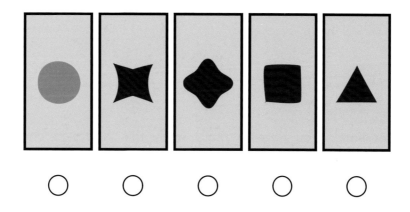

Which picture does not belong with the other pictures?

Hints :

This one takes time! You have to really study the shapes to understand the differences. Think about their color, their shape, their background, and their angle. Is there anything where they are different? Their colors are the same. Their shapes are all different. Their backgrounds are the same. What about their angle? What about the line going through each one? Which way does it go in each shape?

Inspiration :
Alvin Lustig - Princess of cleves /
Artist style

Answers :
Second box starting from the left

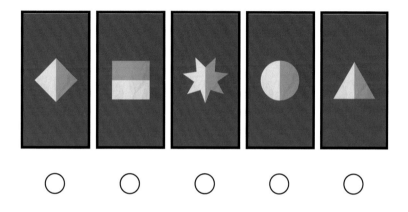

○   ○   ○   ○   ○

Which one of these pictures does not belong with the others?

Hints :

This question is not just about color or shape, it's about what each thing is. What is the first picture a drawing of? What about the others? All of the drawings except for one are of the same kind of thing. What is it? What isn't a drawing of that kind of thing?

Inspiration :
Milton Glaser - Only words, until an
artist uses them

Answers :
Second box starting from the left
on the top row

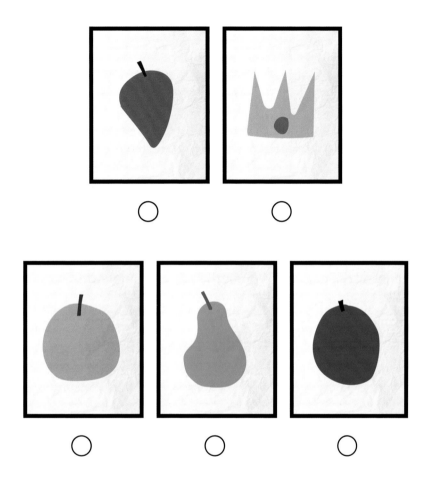

Which one of these pictures does not belong with the others?

Hints :

Start by naming all the animals. What is the same about most of these animals?

Think about animals in different ways. Their color, their shape, what kind of animal they are. Is there anything that seems different about them?

Inspiration :
A.M Cassandre - Pivolo poster /
Artist style

Answers :
Second box starting from the left
on the bottom row

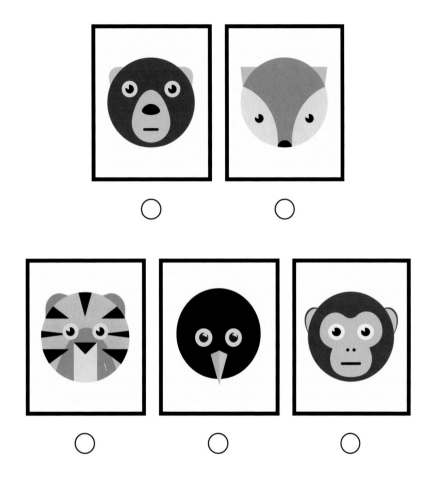

Which one of these pictures does not belong with the others?

Hints :

By "go together" the puzzle is asking you for the ones that are really similar or the same kind of thing. Two of the things are flying vehicles - which two are those?

Inspiration :
Romero Britto - Artist style

Answers :
The rocket on the top left box
and the plane on the bottom right box

Point to the picture on the top row and the picture on the bottom row that go together.

Hints :

By "go together" the puzzle is asking you for the ones that are really similar or the same kind of thing. Two of the things are food and the others aren't. Which two are food?

Inspiration :
Roy Lichtenstein - Artist style

Answers :
The banana on the top left box
and the apple on the bottom left box

Point to the picture on the top row and the picture on the bottom row that go together.

Hints :

1.Go through each picture and ask yourself: is this a fruit? If it isn't, cross it out. What's left?

2.Go through each picture and ask yourself, is this an animal? If it isn't, cross it out.

3.A utensil is another word for a tool we use at meals. Go through each picture and ask yourself, is this a utensil? If it isn't, cross it out. What is left?

Inspiration :
Anna Huskowska - Dumbo

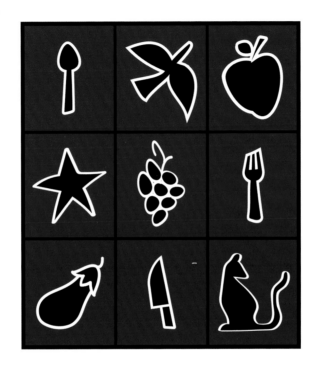

1. There are lots of different things in this picture. Point to all of the fruit.
2. Now point to all of the animals.
3. What about the utensils? Point to all of the utensils in the picture.

Hints :

If you can't find the objects from the question, let's go one by one through each object. What is in the top left corner? A present? Great. What about next to it...

Inspiration :
Henri de toulouse Lautrec
- Your mouth

Answers :
Instruments: The piano on the middle right box, the guitar on the middle left box
Jewelry: The necklace on the bottom left box, the ring on the bottom right box, the necklace on the top middle box

Read each question out loud one time.

1. There are lots of different things in this picture. Point to all of the musical instruments.
2. What about the jewelry? Point to all of the jewelry.

Hints :
Let's start by finding the name of each object.
What is in the top left corner? What is next to it?

Inspiration :
Osvaldo Cavandoli
- La linea

Answers :
Buildings: The house on the top left box, the flat on the
middle right box, the house on the bottom middle box
People: The man on the middle left box,
the woman on the bottom right box
Object that erupts : The volcano on the top middle box

Read each question out loud one time.

1. There are lots of different things in this picture. Point to all of the buildings.
2. What about the people? Point to all of the people.
3. Now can you find the object that erupts? Point to it.

Hints :

1. To find the tools, go one by one through each picture, and ask yourself, is this a tool? If it is put a little check-mark next to it. If it isn't, cross it out.

2. To find the animals, go through each picture and ask yourself, is this an animal? cross out the ones that aren't animals. What's left?

3. To find the deserts, go through each picture one by one and ask yourself: is this a dessert? Cross out the picture if it isn't a dessert. What's left?

Answers :
Tools: The wrench on the top left box, the screwdriver on the top right box, the hammer on the middle left box
Animals: The pig on the bottom left box,
the chicken on the bottom right box
Desserts: The icecream at the middle

Inspiration :
Edel Rodriguez - Protected

Read each question out loud one time.

1. There are lots of different things in this picture. Point to all of the tools.
2. Now point to all of the animals.
3. What about the desserts. Point to all of the desserts in the picture.

Pattern completion

Pattern completion questions ask students to recognize a pattern in a picture and to complete the pattern correctly with a missing piece. A simple version might be to have a picture of a face, missing a nose, and ask which of the answer pictures (one a nose, the others not) should go into the picture. However, usually the tests use abstract shapes in their questions, so we have done the same here.

Pattern recognition involves, most fundamentally, simply getting into the habit of observing pictures and looking for their various patterns. A simple way you can help your child become adept at this is to point them out yourself and enter into conversations about patterns— to look at how a line goes around and around in a circle, or to name together all the colors or shapes in a picture. By observing the picture yourself and verbalizing what aspects of the picture strike you, you can help your child to think along the same lines.

You can also create simple puzzles of your own. Take nine bananas and lay them out in a box in rows of three. Now take a banana away. Ask what goes in the missing spot. If they can answer this question, they are well on their way to understanding pattern recognition questions, and you can make them more complex. Make the pattern with apples. Then make a variegated pattern that goes apple, banana, apple. Now try switching the order around. You get the idea...

Hints :
Which part of the picture is missing?
What color is the part that is missing?

Inspiration :
Donald Judd - Untitled

Answers :
Third box starting from the left

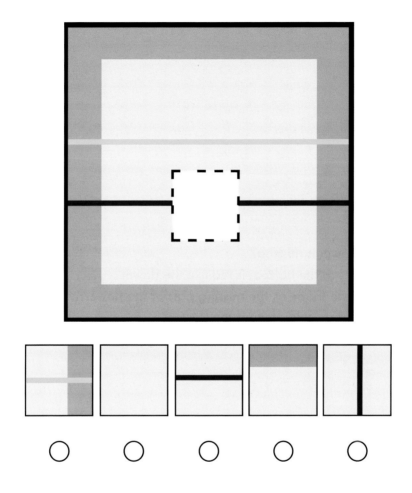

Which of the pictures at the bottom fits into the hole in the painting without changing the pattern?

Hints :

Which part of the flower is missing?

Which of the pictures at the bottom is red like the flower?

Which one is the same shape as the missing part of the flower?

Which one has the same color behind the flower?

Inspiration :
Paul Kremer - **SCANDALE** *Project*

Answers :
Fourth box starting from the left

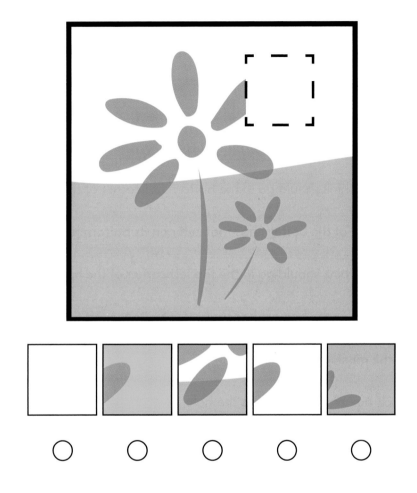

Which of the pictures at the bottom fits into the hole in the painting without changing the pattern?

Hints :

What color boxes are around the missing piece?

What color do you think should go in the bottom left corner of the hole?

Which of the pieces at the bottom has that color on its bottom left part?

What color do you think should go in the top left corner of the hole?

Which of the pieces at the bottom has that color on its top left part?

How big are the missing parts of each box?

If you put each box at the bottom in the hole, which one would make all the boxes stay square?

Inspiration :
Piet Mondrian - Unnamed composition

Answers :
Second box starting from the left

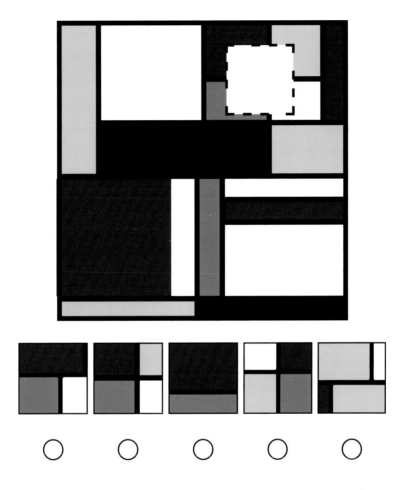

Which of the pieces at the bottom fits into the hole in the painting without changing the pattern ?

Hints :

If you picked up each picture at the bottom and put in the missing spot, which one fits best?

Which one has the lines curving the right way?

Inspiration :
Jasper Johns - Target with
Four Faces

Answers :
Second box starting from the left

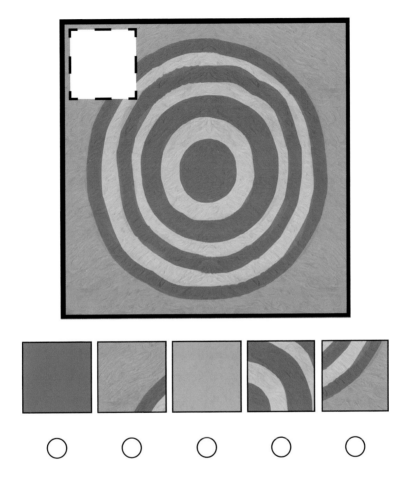

Which of the pictures at the bottom fits into the hole in the painting without changing the pattern?

Hints :

What color boxes are around the missing piece?

What color do you think should go in the bottom left corner of the hole?

Which of the pieces at the bottom has that color on its bottom left part?

What color do you think should go in the top left corner of the hole?

Which of the pieces at the bottom has that color on its top left part?

How big are the missing parts of each box?

If you put each box at the bottom in the hole, which one would make all the boxes stay rectangles?

Inspiration :
Paul Klee - Fartbafel

Answers :
First box starting from the left

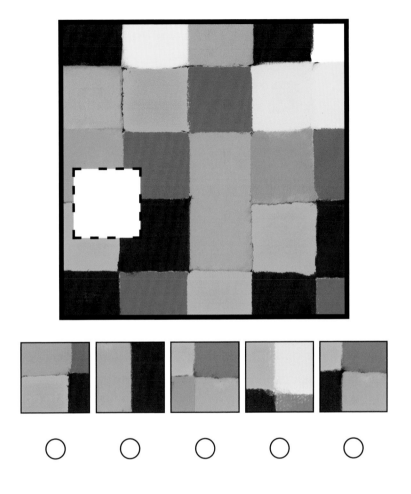

Which of the pieces at the bottom fits into the hole in the painting without changing the pattern ?

75

Hints :

What color do you think should go at the very bottom of the missing part?

What color line would go through the bottom of the missing part if the hole was not there?

What color do you think should go at the very top of the hole?

What order do the colors go in starting at the bottom and going up?

Which of the pieces at the bottom have the lines in the same order?

Do the lines in the picture where the missing part is go from left to right or do they go up and down?

If the missing part were filled in, would the lines go straight or would they bend?

Inspiration :
Frank Stella - Gran Cairo

Answers :
Third box starting from the left

Which of the pictures at the bottom fits into the hole without changing the pattern?

Hints :

Which piece at the bottom has all of those missing parts?

What color do you think should go in the bottom left corner of the hole?

Which of the pieces at the bottom has that color on its bottom left part?

What color do you think should go in the top left corner of the hole?

Which of the pieces at the bottom has that color on its top left part?

Look at the long red rectangle in the middle that is missing a part of it. Which of the boxes at the bottom would finish the red rectangle?

Ask your student: Why did you pick that one? Let them explain to you and then talk about what works and doesn't work.

Inspiration :
Vilmos Huszar - Hammer and saw

Answers :
Fifth box starting from the left

Which of the pictures at the bottom fits into the hole without changing the pattern?

Hints :
Let's look at the colors stripes and how wide they are.

What color stripe is on the far right of the missing box? Which piece at the bottom has that color on the far right?

Which colors should be going through the missing part? What order should they go on? Which piece at the bottom has those colors in that order?

How wide are the stripes? Which of the boxes at the bottom has stripes that are wide in the same way?

If you put each box at the bottom in the hole, which one would make all the stripes stay the same?

Inspiration :
Gene Davis - Sweet score Skylark

Answers :
Fourth box starting from the left

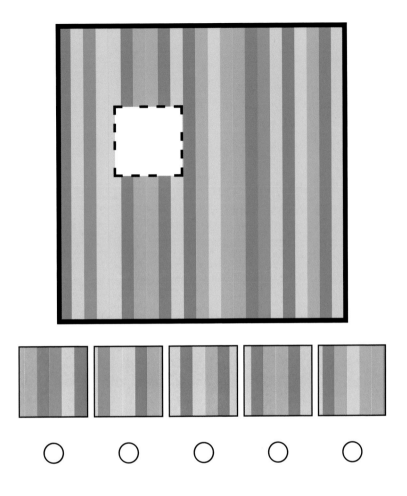

Which of the pictures at the bottom fits into the hole without changing the pattern?

Hints :

What color do you think should go on the right of the missing box? Which piece at the bottom has that color on the right?

What color do you think should go on the bottom left of the missing box? Which piece at the bottom has that color on the bottom left?

Do you think the big yellow rectangle at the bottom goes all the way to the end of the missing box or just part of the way?

Which piece at the bottom has the yellow box doing that?

Can you see the big triangle in the picture? Which piece at the bottom will complete the triangle?

Inspiration :
Carmen Herrera - Tondo3colors

Answers :
Fourth box starting from the left

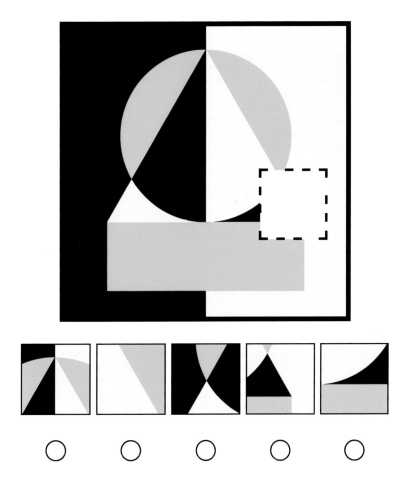

Which of the pictures at the bottom fits into the hole without changing the pattern?

Hints :

Is there a circle that goes through the missing part? Which of the pieces at the bottom would complete the circle?

Are the lines that go through the top of the missing part close together or far apart?

What about the bottom of the box? Which piece at the bottom has lines like that?

How many lines do you think go through the top of the missing box? Which piece at the bottom has the same number of lines going through the top?

Inspiration :
Rakuko Naito - Black Stripes

Answers :
Third box starting from the left

Which of the pictures at the bottom fits into the hole without changing the pattern?

Hints :

What color of the rainbow should go in the top left corner of the missing box?
What should the next color down be?

Which piece at the bottom has those colors there?

What color should go in the bottom right corner of the missing box? Which piece at the bottom has that color in the bottom right corner?

About how much of the missing box do you think should be filled up by the red circle? Which piece has about that much red at its bottom?

Inspiration :
Frank Stella - Haran II

Answers :
Second box starting from the left

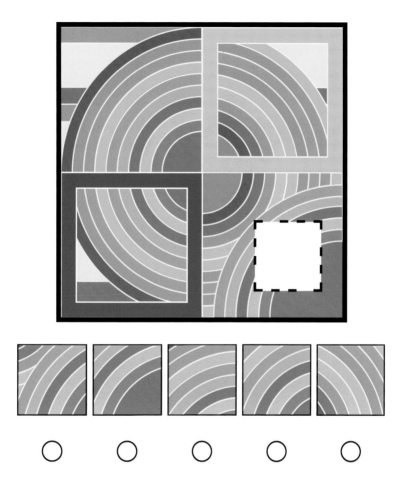

Which of the pictures at the bottom fits into the hole without changing the pattern?

Reasoning by analogy

Reasoning by analogy questions ask children to find the analogy between one set of pictures and another set of pictures. This involves three key steps: (a) finding the pattern in the first set of objects, (b) figuring out how the objects in the other set follow that same pattern, and then (c) figuring out how to make that same pattern with one of the objects in the answer. The questions are asking students to see how analogies can be made on paper with objects in a pattern.

Again, bananas and apples are perfect material for analogy practice. To extend or prepare for the analogy puzzles in this book, simply line up nine bananas in a box in rows of three. Make sure they are all pointed in the same direction. Remove the bottom right corner banana. Ask your child how to place the missing banana.

Now turn all of them so that they are pointing horizontally. Ask your child how he thinks the final banana should be laid down now. Should he place it in a way that is not "correct" this is something to be accepted and talked about. "Oh that is a fun way to place it. How would you place it if you wanted it to look like the other bananas?"

To make it more complex, turn the first row all the way horizontal and the second row partly horizontal. Now leave the third row vertical. How should the missing banana lie?

Now let your child be the puzzle creator and create puzzles for you. Allowing your child to "teach" you their pattern is a great way to empower them to learn how to "think" like a puzzle.

Inspiration :
Miroko Machiko - Artist style

Answers :
Fourth box starting from the left

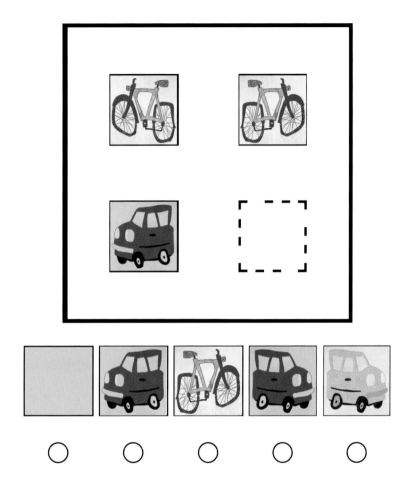

Which of the pictures at the bottom fits into the hole in the painting without changing the pattern?

Hints :

Look at the top row. What changes in the picture from the box on the left to the box on the right? If the same thing happens to the box on the bottom left, what will the new box look like?

Inspiration :
Yayoi Kusama - Once the
Abominable War is Over

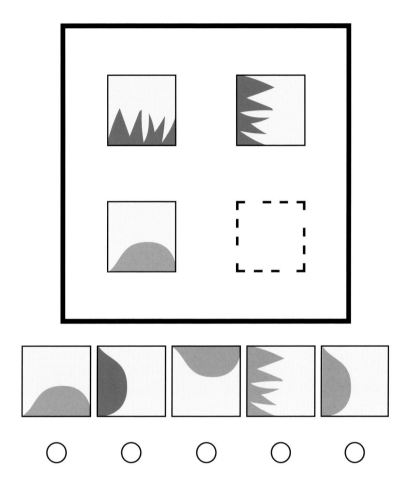

Which of the pictures at the bottom fits into the hole without changing the pattern?

Hints :

What's different about the circles on the top row and the bottom row? Which of the pictures would show that in the missing spot?

Inspiration :
Hilma af Klint- Buddha's
Standpoint in the Earthly Life

Answers :
Third box starting from the left

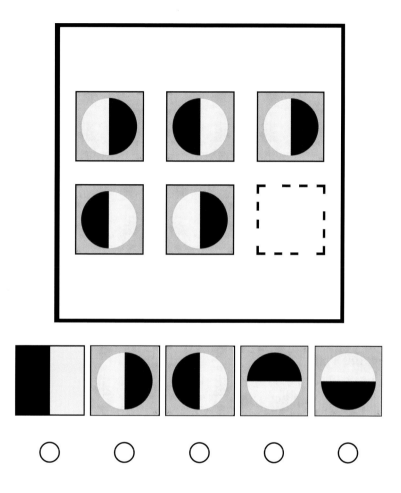

Which of the pictures at the bottom fits into the hole in the painting without changing the pattern?

Hints :

The flower on top has all of its petals.

Which picture shows the bottom flower with all of it's petals?

Inspiration :
Mizuki Goto - Untitled print

Answers :
Fifth box starting from the left

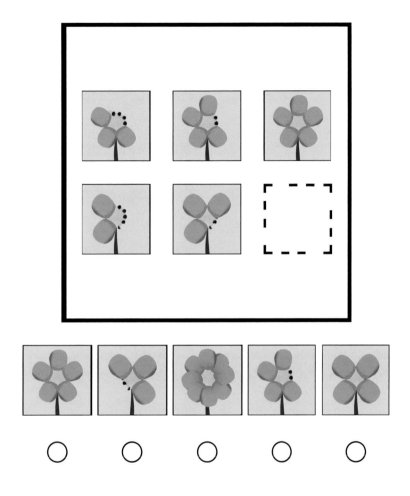

Which of the pictures at the bottom fits into the hole in the painting without changing the pattern?

Hints :
Look at the top row, do you see how the shapes change as they go from left to right? If the bottom row keeps the same pattern, what would the last shape look like?

Look at the puzzle going from top to bottom in each column. What is the difference between the top left shape and the one below it? What about the middle top and the one below it? What about the top right? What should the one below it look like to keep the pattern the same?

Look for clues. Here the clue seems to be the black sticks. How many black sticks are in the top left box? What about the middle box? What about the top right?
Now lets look at the sticks on the bottom. How many on the left? How many in the middle? How many should be on the right?

Inspiration :
Paul Klee - Characters in yellow

Answers :
Third box starting from the left

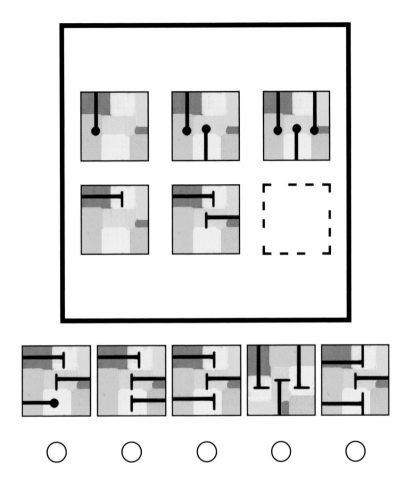

Which of the pictures at the bottom fits into the hole without changing the pattern?

Hints :

We are looking for patterns again. The top row and the bottom row are both going to follow the same pattern, or rule.

How does the circle change as it goes from left to right?

Do you see the circle at the bottom moving in the same way? How does it change from the left to the middle? How might it keep changing if it keeps going the same way?

Lets look for things that are the same between the top and the bottom. On the top left, the circle is green on one side and yellow on the other. What about the bottom, is it split down the middle? Does it turn the same way the one on top turns?

Inspiration :
Vassily Kandinsky - Shallow deep

Answers :
Fifth box starting from the left

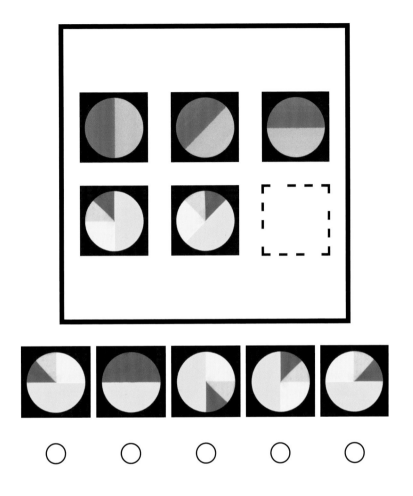

Which of the pictures at the bottom fits into the hole without changing the pattern?

Hints :
This is another relationship game. What is the relationship between the top left and top right box? What changed about the box on the left when it became the box on the right? If the same thing changes on the bottom, what will it look like?

Inspiration :
Kasimir Malevitch -
Suprematism series

Answers :
Fifth box starting from the left

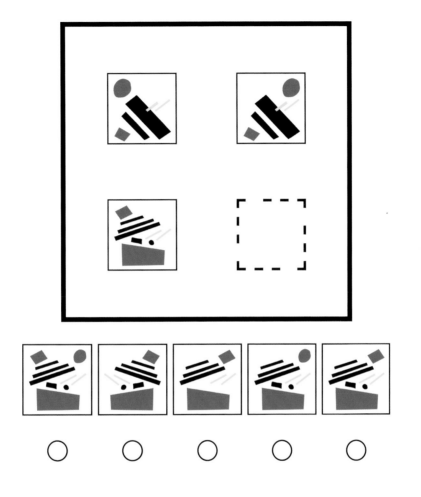

Which of the pictures at the bottom fits into the hole without changing the pattern?

Hints :

The game is to look for patterns or relationships. Do you see a relationship between the top row and the bottom? Look at the boxes on the left top and left bottom. In what ways do they look alike? What about the ones in the middle? If we keep the same pattern, what will the bottom right version of the top right look like?

The boxes on the bottom are just like the ones on top, but are square and on the other side. If we make the top right circle square and flip it to the other side, which answer at the bottom will it look like?

The boxes on the bottom - do they have the dark part on the same side or different? On the top right, which side is the dark part? Which side should the dark part be on the bottom right then?

Inspiration :
Ward Jackson - Untitled
(Concentric)

Answers :
Fourth box starting from the left

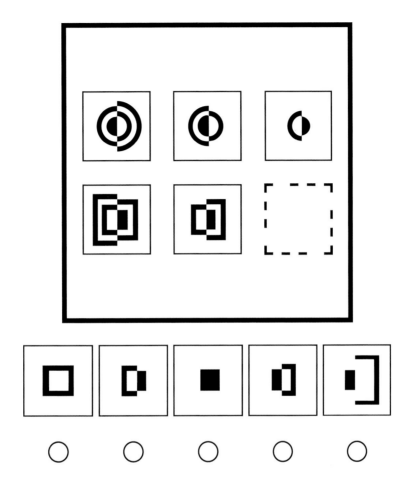

Which of the pictures at the bottom fits into the hole without changing the pattern?

Sequential Reasoning

Sequential Reasoning asks children to look at a series of objects to try to discover the rule that advances the series along. The key difference between sequential reasoning and pattern recognition or analogical reasoning is that sequences tend not to repeat, they advance according to a rule. A very simple sequence is 2, 4, 6, 8, 10. Discovering the secrets of more complicated sequences, such as the Fibonnaci sequence or others, are studied today at the highest levels of university research institutes. The questions on tests for kindergarteners tend to be about finding visual sequences as opposed to mathematical ones. In other words, the sequences rely on a rule that has to do with the color, shape and/or position of the objects in the series.

As always, the best way to continue exploring this type of reasoning is simply to observe the various aspects of the picture-puzzle to point out what is striking to you. Slowly, you can introduce how the shapes that are pictured relate to each other, and let your child show you the ways she sees them as related. This can be as simple as pointing out how an object seems to turn as it goes across the row, or how an object seems to change color. Ask if she sees anything changing. She may very well point out patterns that are not being asked for — that's okay! The more you explore the puzzles in this way, the more your child is likely to understand the types of patterns that you are intuiting — because she too is building up an experience of exploring patterns upon which to intuit.

Again, there are many simple ways to create sequences to practice with beyond this book. One method is to line up all of your child's toy cars or dolls by size. Start with the smallest and work your way up to the largest. Now, find an even larger toy. Ask where it should go. What about a medium toy? Where should it go?

Now ask your child to create a sequence puzzle for you.

Hints :

Pick the picture at the bottom that is the right shape and color!

The top row is all what shape? What about the middle row?
If the bottom row stays the same shape too, what should go in the missing spot?
The left column is all pink. The middle column is all yellow.
What color are the pictures on the right?

Inspiration :
Robert Delaunay - Rythm 1

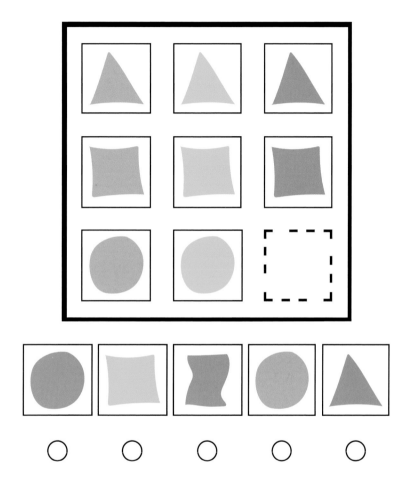

Which of the pictures at the bottom fits into the hole in the painting without changing the pattern?

Hints :

All the cans on the top row are which color? All the cans in the middle row are which color? All the cans on the bottom row should be which color?

Do you see a pattern going down the columns? It goes yellow, green, red. Yellow, green, red. Yellow, green... now what?

This game is about finding patterns. Patterns are colors that repeat. The top row is one pattern where yellow repeats. The next row is another pattern with what color repeating? What about the bottom row. What pattern is that?

Inspiration :
Andy Warhol -
Campbell soup / Marylin Monroe

Answers :
First box starting from the left

110

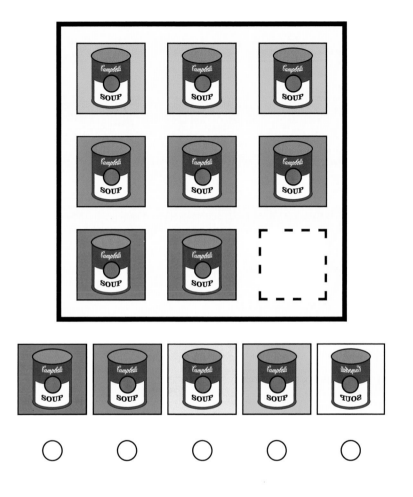

Which of the pictures at the bottom fits into the hole without changing the pattern?

Hints :

Each row has three colors. What color is missing in the bottom row?

Each column has three colors. What color is missing in the last column?

This game is about finding patterns. Patterns are colors that are in order. What is the order of the top row? What is the order of the middle row? What should the order be in the bottom row to keep the pattern the same.

Inspiration :
Andy Warhol - Banana

Answers :
Fifth box starting from the left

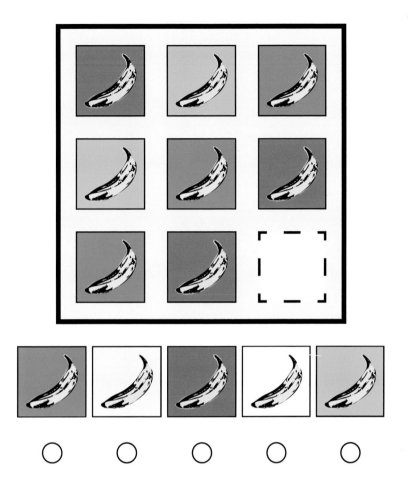

Which of the pictures at the bottom fits into the hole without changing the pattern?

Hints :

What do all the shapes in the top row have in common?

What is different about the top row from the middle row?

What about the bottom row from the middle row?

Look at the color in the background of each shape. What color is the background of the bottom row?

Inspiration :
Vassily Kandinsky - Squares
with concentric circles

Answers :
First box starting from the left

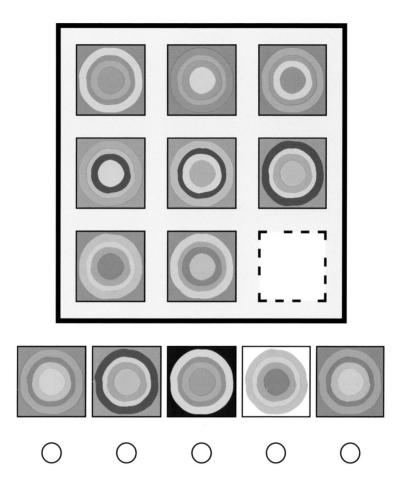

Which of the pictures at the bottom fits into the hole without changing the pattern?

Hints :

This is a pattern game. The key is to figure out what the pattern in each row is, and then to use the same pattern in the last row.

What are the different shapes in the top row? What are the colors? What about the middle row? If we use the same pattern, what is the bottom row missing?

Do colors repeat or not repeat in each row? What colors should not be in the last box on the bottom? Cross those off.

Does any shape and color combination repeat anywhere? If not, cross off any answer choice that shows the shape and color repeating.

What's left?

Inspiration :   *Answers :*
Paul Feeley - Etamin / Gomelza   Fourth box starting from the left

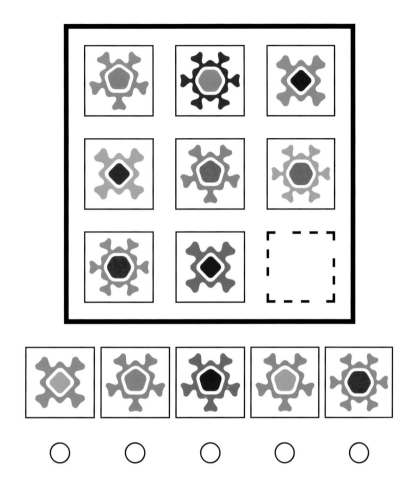

Which of the pictures at the bottom fits into the hole without changing the pattern?

Hints :

Look for patterns in how the shapes change... In the top row, can you see how the ball is changing? How is it changing? Is it changing colors? Is it changing directions? What about the middle row?

What about the bottom row? What colors and directions are missing?

If you go down each column, does the ball change at all? In what ways? Does each column have colors? What about directions? What do you think the last column is missing?

Inspiration :
Marcel Duchamp - Rotorelief

Answers :
Fifth box starting from the left

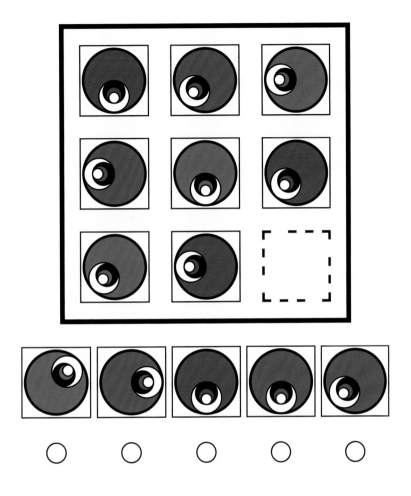

Which of the pictures at the bottom fits into the hole without changing the pattern?

Hints :

How do the red and green pictures change as you go to the right? What would make the purple pictures change the same way?

Inspiration :
Jack Bush - Sea deep

Answers :
First box starting from the left

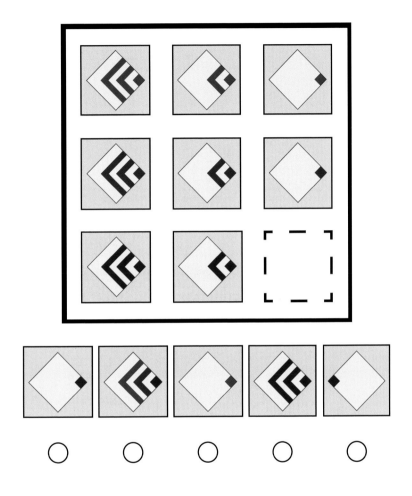

Which of the pictures at the bottom fits into the hole in the painting without changing the pattern?

Hints :
This is a pattern game. Do you see a pattern in the boxes as they go from left to right? Which shape would keep that pattern going?

Inspiration :
Alexander Calder - Red Polygons

Answers :
First box starting from the left

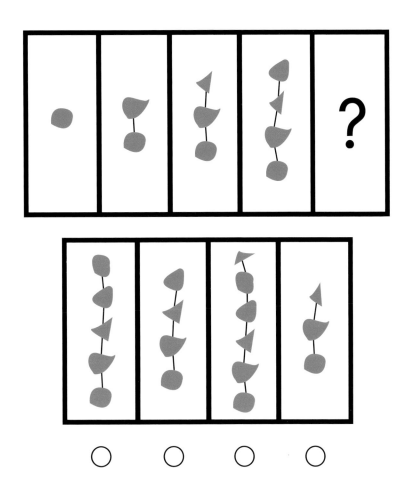

Which of the pictures at the bottom fits into the hole without changing the pattern?

Hints :

Is each box the same or different? Do you think the final box will be the same as one of the other boxes or different? Which answer choice is different than all the other boxes?

Inspiration :
Kasimir Malevitch -
Suprematism series

Answers :
Second box starting from the left

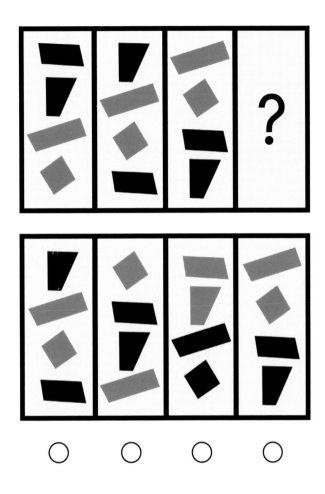

Which of the pictures at the bottom fits into the hole without changing the pattern?

Hints :

The black lines seem to be filling up more and more of the box. Which picture at the bottom fills up the whole box the same way?

Each box has big lines and little lines in it. Which of the pictures at the bottom has big lines and little lines the same way?

Inspiration :
John McLaughlin - Untitled

Answers :
Second box starting from the left

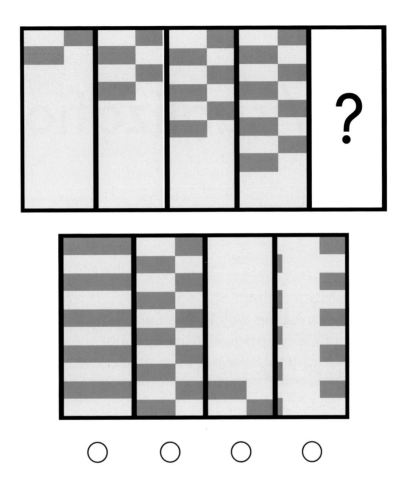

Which of the pictures at the bottom fits into the hole in the painting without changing the pattern?

Spatial Visualization

Spatial Visualization questions challenge students to imagine how shapes would look if they were changed in some way that is suggested, but is not directly made on the paper. For example, a question might ask what a rectangle might look like if it was folded in half, or might ask what two objects would look like if one was partly in front of the other.

Again, we encourage you to talk about the puzzles and what you see in them as a way to generate conversation about them with your child. Usually, there is a set of pictures that shows an example of what the question asks of your child. Talk about the example in detail. What is going on? How do you verbalize that? How might they? This gives children a language for expressing what they see and gives you a chance to guide their thoughts toward what is being asked of them.

Spatial visualization is a skill that is also easy to practice at home. One way is with a piece of cardboard that you can cut into the shape of a cube. What shape do you have to cut it into so that all the sides of the cube will be there when you fold it up? By making a cube of cardboard with your child you can begin to explore the relationship between the 3D world and the 2D world. You can then paint a house on the cube, and encourage your child to make a whole town. Again, allow your child the chance to be the task creator. Ask him what kind of house he wants you to create, and create it in front of him. Of course there are so many more ways. Build objects with popsicle sticks like bridges for their toy cars, or little wooden animals. Work with papier-mâché. Simply encouraging your children to draw an object in front of them is a fascinating and well proven way to encourage their visual spatialization skills.

Hints :
Somebody put the motorcycle back together. Which picture shows what it would look like if someone put the truck back together the same way?

Inspiration :
Lajos Kassák - The Charnel-House

Answers :
Fourth box starting from the left

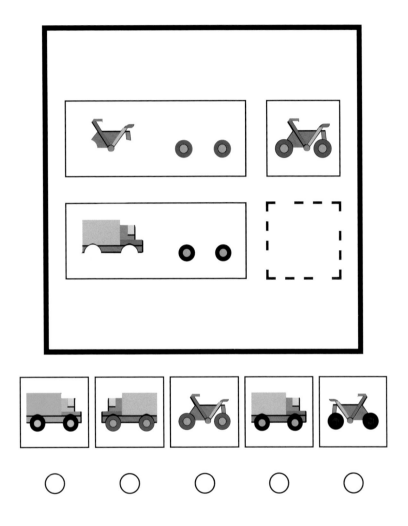

Which of the pieces at the bottom fits into the hole in the painting without changing the pattern?

131

Inspiration :
Anna Huskowska - Dumbo poster

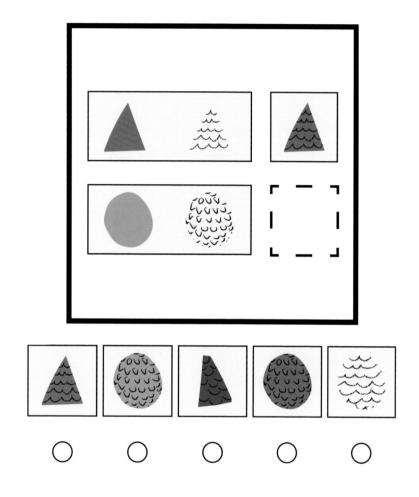

Which of the pieces at the bottom fits into the hole in the painting without changing the pattern?

Hints :
The yellow claw picked up the blue egg. Which picture shows the red claw picking up the green egg the same way?

Inspiration :
Vasily Zvyozdochkin - Original
russian dolls set

Answers :
Second box starting from the left

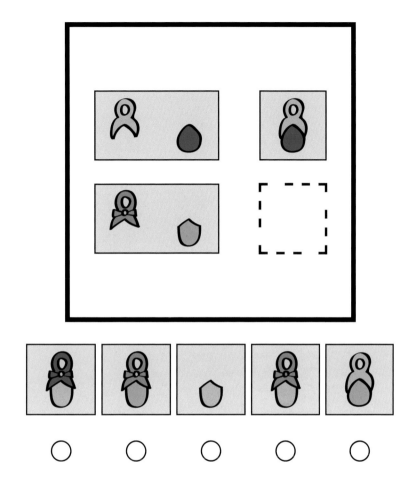

Which of the pieces at the bottom fits into the hole in the painting without changing the pattern?

Hints :
It looks like the top head turned over to eat!
Which picture shows what it would look like if the bottom head turned over to eat the same way?

Inspiration :
Mike Kelley - Animal self and friend
of animal

Answers :
Fourth box starting from the left

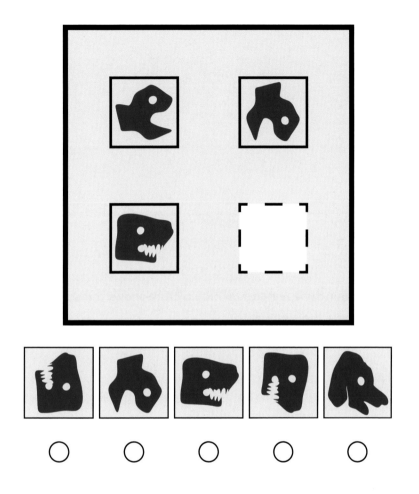

Which of the pictures at the bottom fits into the hole without changing the pattern?

Hints :
The purple star is behind the red star. Which picture shows the purple triangle hiding behind the red triangle the same way?

Inspiration :
Mimmo Castellano - Old posters /
Artist style

Answers :
Third box starting from the left

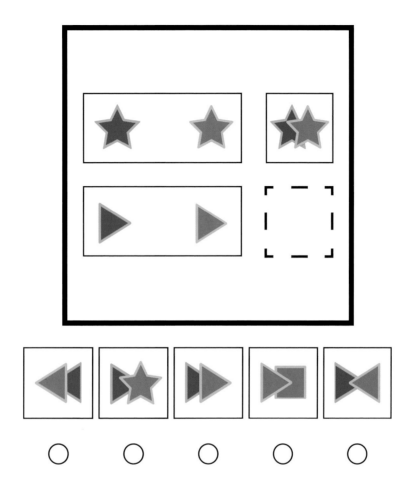

Which of the pictures at the bottom fits into the hole without changing the pattern?

Hints :

The bear is hiding behind the pink pig. Which picture shows what it would look like if the cat hid behind the monkey the same way?

Inspiration :
Junzo Terrada - A good home for
Max / Artist Style

Answers :
Fourth box starting from the left

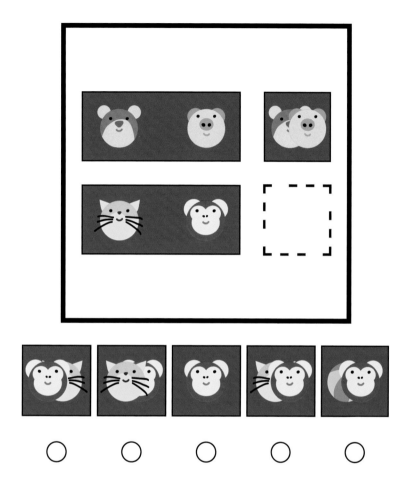

Which of the pictures at the bottom fits into the hole without changing the pattern?

Hints :

If you combined the white and black shapes the same way as the shapes above them, which picture would it look like?

Inspiration :
Jean Arp - Bouteille et oiseau

Answers :
First box starting from the left

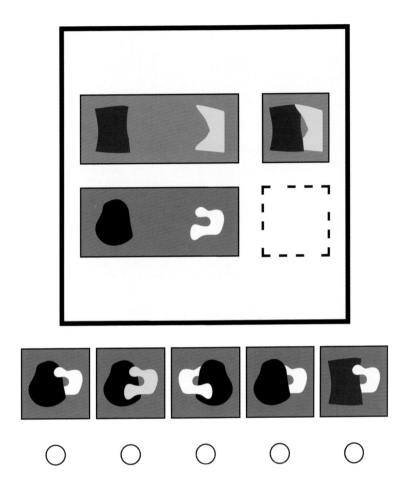

Which of the pictures at the bottom fits into the hole without changing the pattern?

Hints :

The pink shape on the top left was folded into the box on the top right.
If the blue shape on the bottom was folded into a box, what would it look like?

If you only folded the top of the blue down, what would it look like? Which picture is closest to that?

How many blue hills are on top of the box? Which piece at the bottom has the same number of upside down hills?

Are the blue hills in the middle or on one side of the box? Which piece at the bottom has the hills in the same place?

About how big are the blue hills? Which piece on the bottom has upside down hills about the same size?

If you drew the hills folded up, what would it look like? Draw it!

Inspiration :
Henri Matisse - The wave (La vague)

Answers :
Fifth box starting from the left

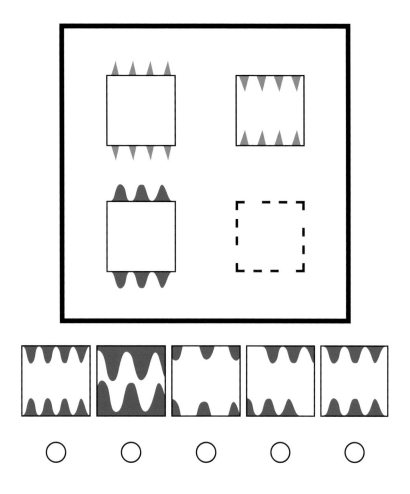

Which of the pictures at the bottom fits into the hole without changing the pattern?

Hints :

Look at the left side of the box. If you folded in just this side, what would it look like?

Which of the pieces on the bottom looks like that?

What about the bottom of the shape? If you folded up the bottom of the shape, what would it look like? Which of the pieces on the bottom looks like that?

Can you draw what it would look like if you folded each part of the shape into the box? Draw it! Which piece on the bottom looks like that?

Inspiration :
Henri Matisse - Artist style

Answers :
Third box starting from the left

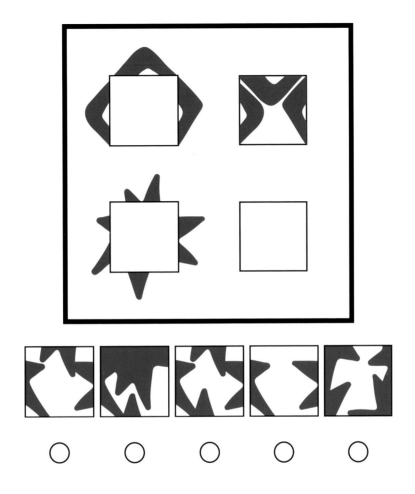

The shape on the top left was folded into the box on the top right. If you folded the shape on the bottom left into the box on the right, what would it look like?

Hints :

If the shape on the bottom was folded into a box, what would it look like?

Part of the shape on the top left is folded in on the top right. If you folded in the shape on the bottom left, what would it look like?

How big is the box? If you put the empty box on the right on top of the box on the left, what would stick out?

If you folded in the part that sticks out what would the left part of the box look like? What color is the right of the box? What piece on the bottom has that color on the right side?

How long is the rectangle on the left? If you folded it in would it go all the way down the side or part of the way down the side?

Inspiration :
Piet Mondrian - Composition C

Answers :
Third box starting from the left

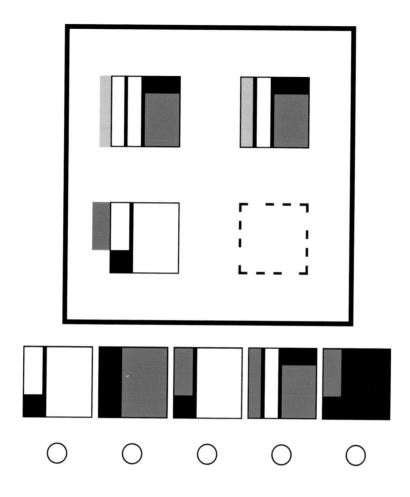

The shape on the top left was folded into the box on the top right.

If you folded the shape on the bottom left into the box the same way what would it look like?

Hints :

The 3 pieces on the top form a pattern. So do the 3 pieces on the bottom. How should we finish the pattern on the bottom so that it has the same rules as the pattern on top?

What are the rules for the patten on top? In the first box on the top there is one triangle, in the second box there is another triangle? What about the third box on top? How many triangles are there?

If you drew in what you thought the missing box should look like, what would it look like? Draw it!

The top row has both blue triangles in the third box. If both black triangles were in the third box, what would it look like?

Inspiration :
Theo Van Doesburg - Counter
composition V

Answers :
Second box starting from the left

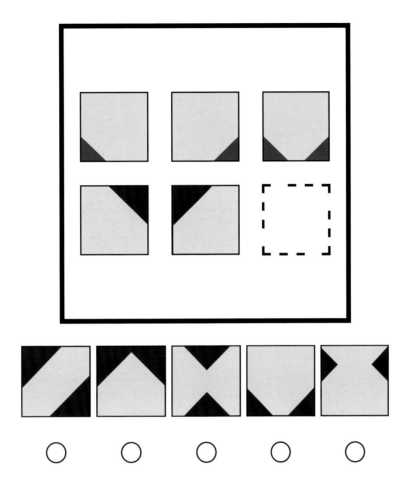

Which of the pictures at the bottom fits into the hole without changing the pattern?

Hints :

The shape on the top left was folded into the box on the top right.
If the shape on the bottom was folded into a box, what would it look like?

If you only folded the red part on the left in, what would it look like? Which picture is closest to that?

About how big is the red shape on the right. Which picture at the bottom has it about the same size?

Are the red shapes in the middle at the top or on the bottom. Which picture has the red shapes at the same height?
If you drew the shape folded up, what would it look like? Draw it!

Inspiration :
Alexander Calder - On yellow

Answers :
Fourth box starting from the left

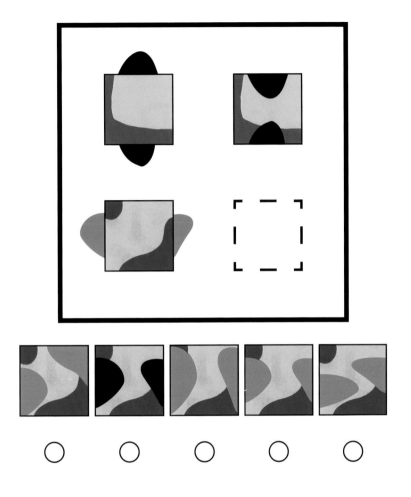

Which of the pictures at the bottom fits into the hole without changing the pattern?

Quantitative Reasoning

Quantitative Reasoning questions are of course, one of the foundations of math, and so neatly maps onto our common notion of math that they probably need far less of an explanation. This is the reasoning that asks questions such as "if we have three dogs and we take away 2, how many are left?"

Some types of quantitative reasoning questions ask children to perform two steps of math. For instance, some questions ask "if I had three cookies and took away one, but then added four, how many would I have?"

The third form of quantitative reasoning questions asks about mathematical language (doubling, halving etc.) and the fourth asks children to group numbers together, such as "If i have two nests and each nest has three birds how many do I have?"

To explore these skills further, you can integrate this into daily life by including them in your daily calculations. Simple questions about grocery shopping cut right to the reasoning tested: "How many objects did you buy today at the grocery store? What if we hadn't bought the cheesecake and the napkins? How many would we have bought then?" Of course, you can then add complexity to your daily life questions as well: "What if I then bought an eggplant. How many things would I now have bought?"

We also suggest exploring these skills through drawings and manipulable objects. Perhaps sometime when you are drawing with your child, ask if he or she would like to do a "math puzzle." Try drawing two trees, each with three apples. Count the apples together. Now ask, "If I drew another tree with two apples, how many would I have?"

You can of course do this with anything — birds with two worms, dogs with four legs, chickens with two legs... Or explore the world around you — if you each bring three toys into the room, how many toys do you have? Now what if another family member brings three toys?

Hints :
Try drawing two black ducks behind each yellow duck.
Now count them up!

Inspiration :
Tomoko Murakami - Ducks
on green background

Answers :
1) Two ducks
2) First box starting from the left

○   ○   ○   ○

1. How many ducks are in the top box?

2. If two black ducks followed each yellow duck, how many black ducks would be following?

Hints :

Draw the number of algae plants Oscar eats. Now draw the number of plants Boscar eats. Now count them all up!

Inspiration :
Élisabeth Ivanovsky - Les très petits

Answers :
First box starting from the left

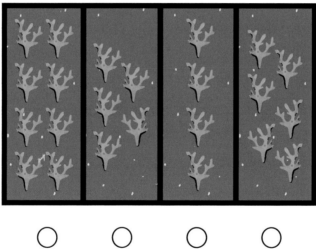

○   ○   ○   ○

This is Oscar and Boscar. They are fish. Each one eats four algae plants for lunch. How many plants do they eat altogether?

Hints :

This is a math game. Each nest has two birds, so draw two birds on top of each nest.
Now count up all the birds. How many birds are there?

Use your imagination! If each nest has two birds, you can imagine each has a mommy
and a daddy. So how many mommies would there be? How many daddies? Which
box at the bottom has the most birds? Count them to see if it has the right number of
daddy birds and mommy birds.

Inspiration :
Basquiat - Basquiat drawings

Answers :
Fourth box starting from the left

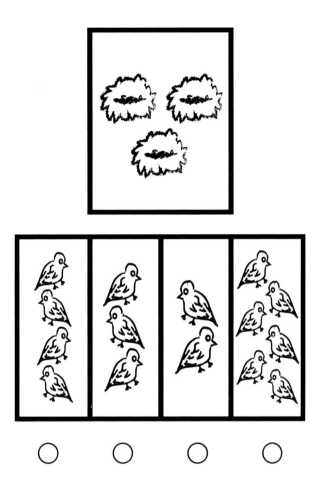

Those are bird nests in the top box. If each nest had two birds in it, how many birds would there be?

Hints :

Draw the number of eggs she lays in the spring. Now draw the number she lays in the summer.

Count them up!

Inspiration :
Nicholas Wilton - Artist style

Answers :
Fourth box starting from the left

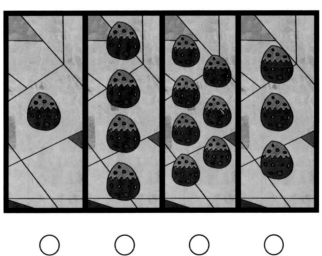

○   ○   ○   ○

This is Susie the Dinosaur. Each spring she lays two eggs, and each summer she lay one egg. She does not lay eggs in winter or fall. How many eggs does she lay all year?

Hints :

1. If you want to figure out how to add dogs, you can draw in each dog you want to add. Now count them up. How many dogs are there?

2. If you want to double the number of dogs, draw a new dog next to each dog that is there. Now count them up. How many dogs are there?

3. If you want to halve the number of dogs, draw a line through the middle of the drawing so that half the dogs are on each side . Now count up how many dogs are on one side?

Inspiration :
Picasso - The Dog

Answers :
1) Second box starting from the left
2) Fourth box starting from the left
3) Third box starting from the left

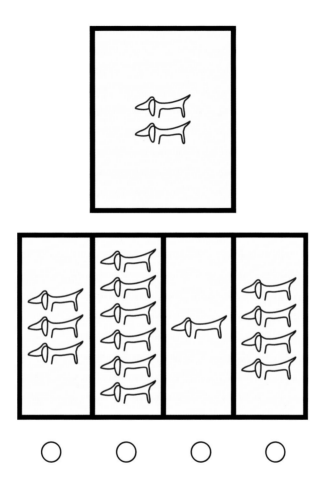

1. How many dogs are in the top box? How many dogs would there be if four more dogs were added? Point to the box with that many dogs at the bottom.

2. What if we doubled the number of dogs in the top box? How many dogs would there be? Point to the box with that many dogs at the bottom.

3. What if we halved the number of dogs in the top box. How many would there be? Point to the box with that many dogs at the bottom.

Hints :

1. To add suns, draw a sun for every sun you will add. Now count up all the suns. How many are there?

2. To double the number of suns, draw a sun next to each sun in the top box. Now how many are there?

3. To triple the number of suns, draw two suns next to each sun in the top box. Now how many suns are there?

Inspiration :
Keith Harring - Inflatable baby
/ Artist style

Answers :
1) First box starting from the left
2) Third box starting from the left
3) Second box starting from the left

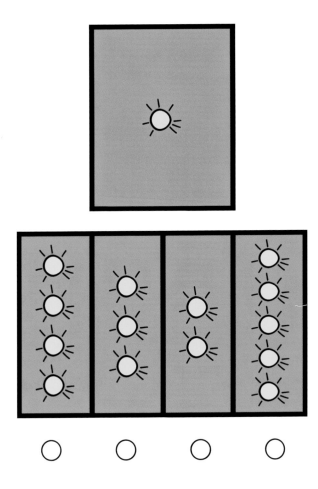

1. In the top box there is a sun. How many would there be if we added 3 suns? Point to the box at the bottom that shows this many suns.

2. What if we doubled the number of suns in the top box. How many suns would there be?

3. What if the sun in the top box tripled? How many suns would there be?

Hints :

1. Adding a crown to the top is like drawing another crown in the top box. Draw a crown in the top box. Now count up the crowns. How many do you have?

2. Subtracting a crown is like crossing out a crown. Take the original 3 crowns. Now cross out one crown. Count them up. How many crowns are left?

3. In this 3rd question, you have to do 2 things. First, draw in a crown to add it. Now, cross out 2 crowns from all the crowns. Now count them up. How many are left?

Inspiration :
Basquiat - Signature / Main symbol

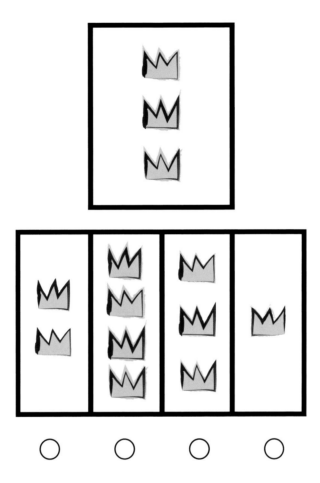

1. There are 3 crowns in the top box. How many crowns would there be if we added a crown?
Point to the box at the bottom which shows that many crowns.
2. What if one crown was subtracted from the box of 3 crowns?
How many crowns would there be then?
3. What if one crown was added to the 3 crowns at the top, and then two crowns were subtracted?
How many crowns would be left?

Hints :

1. Subtracting. Imagine three penguins walked away. How many would be left?

2. Halving: What does it mean to halve? It means to cut in half. If we cut in half the box at the top, how many penguins would be in each half? Draw it? Focus on making sure the line is in the middle from top to bottom.

3. Take these steps one at a time. First subtract. If you cross out 3 penguins, how many are there? Now draw one penguin in to add a penguin. How many do you have?

Inspiration :
Picasso - The Penguin

Answers :
1) Fourth box starting from the left
2) Second box starting from the left
3) Second box starting from the left

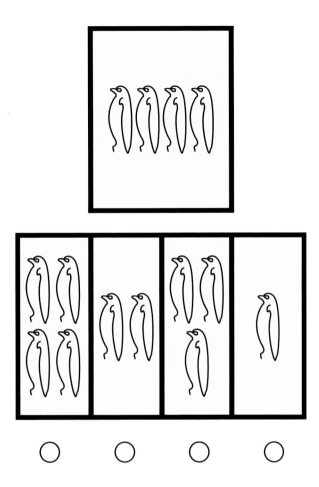

1. In the box on top there are four penguins. If we subtracted three penguins, how many penguins would be left?

2. What if we halved the number of penguins in the top box. How many would be left?

3. If three penguins were taken away from the top box, but then one penguin was put back, how many would there be?

Hints :

To help you figure it out, draw three cookies next to each ice cream cone. Now, how many cookies do you have?

To double something, you can draw two cookies for every donut. Now how many cookies do you have?

Inspiration :
Roy Lichtensein - Sunrise
/ Artist style

Answers :
1) Third box starting from the left
2) Second box starting from the left

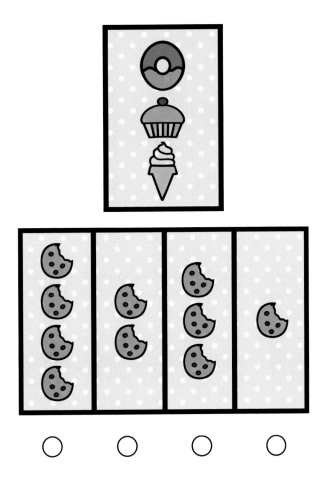

In the top box there is a donut, a cupcake and an ice cream cone.

1. If you had three cookies for every one cupcake, how many cookies would you have?

2. What if you had double the number of cookies that you have donuts. How many cookies would you have?

Aural Comprehension

Aural Comprehension questions test students' ability to remember a series of spoken directions and apply it to a puzzle at hand. For instance, a story might be read aloud about different characters liking different things (Adam likes bananas, Sarah likes apples, and Susie likes avocados). Then children would be asked to link each character with a picture of what the character likes. The directions may become more complex, or may focus on different types of knowledge — such as the ability to understand aural directions about objects, letters, shapes and numbers.

It is important to note that because aural comprehension questions test listening skills, these questions are only read one time. You don't have to practice this way initially, but it's wise to eventually work toward preparing your child that you will only be reading the story once, and then they will be asked about it.

To help children develop specific skills in aural comprehension, or following complex directions, there are many daily tasks which can be relied on. At the grocery store you can tell your child only one time what is on your grocery list and see what he can remember to grab from the different aisles. As you play this more and more he will develop his own devices for remembering. Or perhaps try to cook but only tell your child the recipe one time. See what you create! Involving them in real world tasks that are tactile and with real consequences is a great way to build interest and have fun with even straight-forward memory skills.

Hints :

This is a memory game. To help you remember who wants what, look at the animal as you hear the story and imagine them doing the activity.

Inspiration :
Albert Aquino - Artist style

Answers :
Eat: First box starting from the left
Sleep: Second box starting from the left
Play: Third box starting from the left

Read out loud one time.

A monkey is hungry and wants to eat. A tiger is happy and wants to play. And an elephant is tired and wants to sleep.
Point to the animal that wants to eat. Who wants to sleep? Who wants to play?

Hints :

This is a memory game. Listen carefully! When you hear the question say it out loud again to yourself to help you remember.

Inspiration :
Wojciech Zamecznik - 4 horse heads

Answers :
Second box starting from the left

Read out loud one time:
Lucas was walking in the woods. He was looking for a rabbit but he could not find one.
He did see a dear. Thankfully, he did not see a lion. Point to the picture of what he saw in the forest.

Hints :
This is a memory game. Listen carefully! When you hear the question say it out loud again to yourself to help you remember.

Inspiration :
Unknown- Vintage russian
matchboxes

Answers :
First box starting from the left

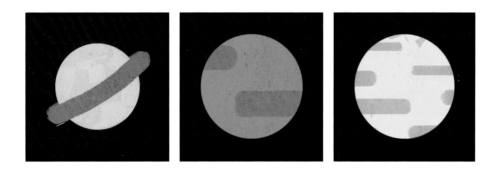

Read out loud one time:

Tommy was an astronaut flying through space.

His rocket flew past the earth, which is blue.

It was now close to Saturn, which has a ring.

It was still far away from Jupiter.

Point to the picture of which planet his rocket was closest to.

Hints :

1. Can you find the boxes where she is wearing a crown? Which one has no bowtie?

2. Can you find the boxes where she is wearing a bowtie? Which one has a hat?

Inspiration :
William Wondriska -
A cat can't count

Answers :
1) Bottom row second box starting from the left
2) Bottom row first box starting from the left

Read each question below one time:

1. This doggy is wearing a disguise! Point to the picture where she is wearing a crown with no bow-tie.
2. Now point to the picture where she is wearing a bow-tie and a hat.

Hints :

1. If you can't find the swan, which animal must it be? Is it the yellow one? The red one? The blue one? Which one is left?

2. Which box has the fish on the right. Now, which of these boxes has a cat next?

3. What color is the bird? Which box doesn't have that one?

Inspiration :
Paul Rand - Animal silouhettes

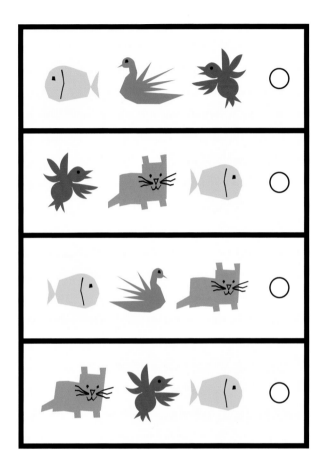

1. Point to the box that has a swan in the middle of a fish and a cat?
2. Now point to the box that has a fish on the right, then a cat, then a bird.
3. Now point to the box without a bird.
4. Now point to the box without a cat.

Hints :

1. A row is a series of boxes that goes from left to right. There are 3 rows. Can you find them?

2. A column is a series of boxes that goes from top to bottom. There are 2 columns. Can you find them?

3. "Right hand" means right...

Inspiration :
Saul Bass - Movie posters
/ Artist style

Answers :
1) Third box starting from the left
2) Second box starting from the left
3) Fourth box starting from the left

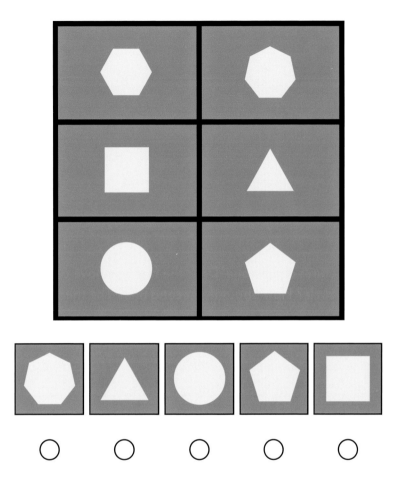

1. Which shape is in the third row, first column? Point to it on the answers at the bottom.
2. Which shape is in the middle row in the second column? Point to it in the answers at the bottom.
3. Which shape is in the right-bottom corner? Point to it in the answers at the bottom.

Hints :

1. Go through the pictures one by one. Does the first one have a triangle on top of a triangle on top of a circle? How about the second one? The third?

2. Which drawings have pink triangles? Which one doesn't have a circle?

Inspiration :
Vassily Kandinsky -
Sketch for picture XVI

Answers :
1) Bottom row first box starting from the left
2) Bottom row second box starting from the left

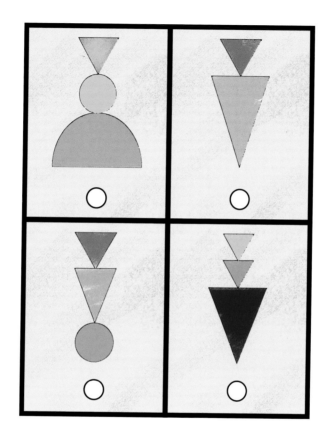

1. Point to the drawing with a triangle on top of a triangle on top of a circle.
2. Now point to the drawing with a pink triangle and no circles.

Hints :

1. Start by finding a circle inside a square. Which shape has that? Now what shape is the square inside? Is that it?

2. Which shape has a square on the outside? What does it have on the inside?

3. Start by finding the plus that is outside a triangle. Can you find it? Now check, is that plus inside a square?

Answers :

1) Bottom row first box starting from the left

2) Top row first box starting from the left

1) Bottom row second box starting from the left

Inspiration :
Kasimir Malevitch - Suprematism series

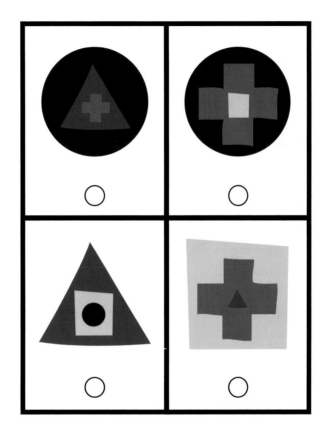

Three Questions:

1. Point to the shape that has a circle inside a square inside a triangle.
2. Now point to the square that has a circle outside a triangle, with a plus in the middle of the triangle.
3. Which shape has a plus that is outside a triangle and inside a square?

Hints :

Can you find an arrow pointing to the left at a number? Which box is this in? Now, in that box, is there an arrow pointing to the right at a letter?

Inspiration :
Henri Matisse -
Typography / Cutouts

Answers :
Top row second box starting from the left

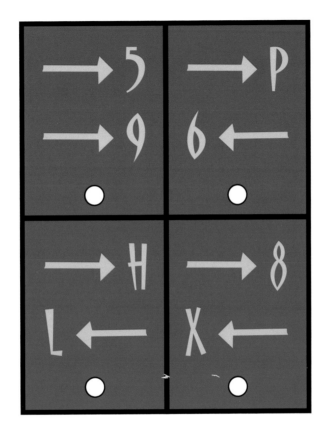

Read out loud one time:

Point to the box with one arrow pointing to the left at a number and one arrow pointing to the right at a letter.

Hints :

Let's start by saying the name of each picture. Now let's go one by one - who puts out fires? Do dinosaurs put out fires? Flowers? What about firemen? Now who knocks down buildings? Let's go one by one.

Answers :
1) The firefighter on the top left box
2) The bulldozer on the middle left box
3) The dinosaur on the top middle box
4) The bird on the middle right box
5) The bulldozer on the middle left box
6) The dog at the middle,
the firefighter on the top left box,
the little girl on the bottom right box

Inspiration :
Picasso - One line drawings

1. Point to the picture of something that puts out fires.
2. Point to the picture of something that knocks down buildings.
3. Point to the one that only lived a long time ago.
4. Point to the one that can fly.
5. Point to the one that is a truck.
6. Point to the ones that are mammals.

Hints :

How can you tell which pictures of the man have his eyes open?

Inspiration :
Henri Matisse - Face on a Yellow
Background

Read out loud each question one time.

1. Point to the picture or pictures of the man where we can see that his eyes are open.

2. Now point to the picture of the man wearing glasses in the top row.

3. Point to the picture of the man with his eyes closed in the middle row where you can't see his hands.

Hints :

1. Go through each picture and ask yourself: is this a vehicle? If it isn't, cross it out. What's left?

2. Go through each picture and ask yourself, is this a drink?

3. Go through each picture and ask yourself, does this live in the ocean? If it doesn't, cross it out. What is left?

Answers :
Vehicles: The truck on the top middle box,
the plane at the middle
Drinks: The bottle on the bottom left box,
the cup on the bottom right box
Things that live in the ocean: The fish on the top left
box, the octopus on the middle right box

Inspiration :
Edward Ruscha -
HONK / Artist style

Read out loud each question one time.

1. Point to all of the vehicles in the painting.

2. Now point to all of the drinks.

3. Point to the pictures of things that live in the ocean.

Aural Reasoning

Aural Reasoning is similar to aural comprehension, but involves hearing a set of conditions and then working to discover those conditions on the page. It is less a task of sole auditory memory and more a combined task of memory and reasoning. For example, a student might be asked aloud to find, amidst many shapes on the page, the place where a triangle is inside a circle, which is inside a square. This involves remembering what was asked, and then searching for this specific condition.

When helping students learn the art of aural reasoning questions, it can be helpful to have children draw information as they learn it. Of course they will not be able to do this on test day, but they will learn the steps required in remembering complex information.

As always, a great way to encourage the growth of this skill in your child is to bring this challenge to real world activities. At the grocery store, you can relay a complex set of instructions for a specific item — for example "bring back the beans that are not white in a can that is not yellow." At home, when cooking, you can again try out multistep aural reasoning, by explaining cooking directions only one time, in abstract ways: "Combine the dry ingredients in one bowl and the wet ingredients in another."

A second form of aural reasoning tested by some private schools and on the Kindergarten Readiness Test (though usually not on gifted and talented tests) is an understanding of metaphor. Students are given basic metaphorical expressions, like "Jack is a couch potato," or "the classroom was a zoo" and tested to see if they can understand the underlying meaning of the metaphor. Using metaphors in daily life with your child is an easy and fun way to teach the concept to them.

Hints :

This is a listening and memory game. To help you remember, when you are listening to the story, find the picture that matches. When you hear "Daddy Kragie brought food" - find it right away! And then say to yourself, that's Daddy Kraggie's!

The same for Mommy Kraggie, when you hear "Mommy Kraggie brought something to lie down on" - find it on the picture and then say to yourself - that's Mommy Kraggie's!

Inspiration :
Paul Rand - Animal
illustrations / Artist style

Answers :
1) The apple on the top right corner
2) The beach towel on the bottom left corner
3) The puzzle piece on the bottom right corner
4) The cat on the top left corner

Read out loud one time.

The Kraggies are off to the park! Each of them brought something...Daddy Kraggie brought food. Mommy Kraggie brought something to lie down on. Lukie Kraggie brought a game. Pamela Kraggie brought her pet.
Point to what Daddy brought. Now point to what Mommy brought. What did Lukie bring? And Pamela, what did she bring?

Hints :

This is another memory game. Listen carefully! When the question is read, say it out loud again to yourself to help you remember.

Inspiration :
Ingela P. Arrhenius - Animals book

Read out loud one time:

Susie asked her mom for a new pet that was not a dog.

The animal she asked for jumps very high and loves eating carrots. Point to the animal she wanted.

Hints :

This is a listening and memory game. To help you remember, when you are listening to the story, find the picture that matches. When you hear "Daddy Kragie brought something to read" - find it right away! And then say to yourself, that's Daddy Kraggie's book.

The same for Mommy Kraggie, when you hear "Mommy Kraggie brought something to drink" - find tit on the picture and then say to yourself - that's Mommy Kraggie's!

Answers :
1) *Mommy brought the bottle on the bottom right corner*
2) *Daddy brought the book on the top right corner*
3) *Lukie brought the toy on the top left corner*
4) *Pamela brought the shovel on the bottom left corner*

Inspiration :
Piet Mondrian - Composition 2

Read out loud one time.

The Kraggies are going to the beach! Each of them brought something special...
Daddy Kraggie brought something to read. Mommy Kraggie brought something to drink. Lukie Kraggie brought a toy. Pamela Kraggie brought something to dig with.
Point to what Mommy brought. Point to what Daddy brought. Point to what Lukie brought. What did Pamela bring?

Hints :

This is a memory game to see if you can remember what the story says. Listen carefully when the question is read again. After you hear the question, say it to yourself out loud.

Inspiration :
Keith Harring - Artist Style

Answers :
Third box starting from the left

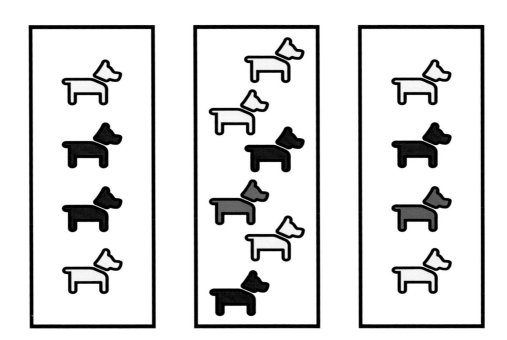

Read this out loud one time:
Anthony was excited because his dog just had four puppies. Two of the puppies were white. One was black. One was brown. Point to the picture of Anthony's new puppies.

Hints :

Sally and Lucy can only paint things they agree on.

Sally didn't want to paint a vehicle - so cross out any vehicles you see.

Lucy didn't want to paint anything yellow, so cross out anything yellow.

What's left?

Inspiration :

Jared chapman- Drawing of a dog

Answers :

Third box starting from the left

Read out loud one time:

Lucy and Sally were going to paint together.

Lucie wanted to paint a firetruck, but Sally didn't want to paint a vehicle.

Sally wanted to paint a Sunflower, but Lucy didn't want to paint anything yellow. Finally they agreed on one of the above. Point to the painting they made.

Hints :

Let's go shape by shape. Is the blue triangle inside both circles? What about the red star? What about the square? The yellow blob? The green rectangle?

Inspiration :
Paul Rand - IBM Campaign
/ Artist style

Answers :
1) Fifth box starting from the left
2) First box starting from the left

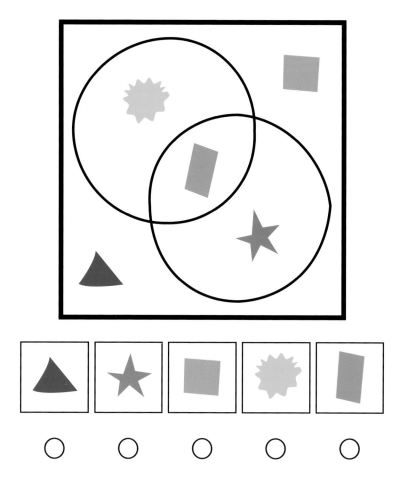

1. Point to the picture on the bottom which shows the shape that is between both circles.
2. Now point to the picture on the bottom that shows a shape that is not in either circle and is not a square.

Hints :

These are memory questions - as the question is only told once to students. To help students remember, it's helpful to teach them to draw what they are hearing as they hear it. So they can draw a circle on top of a square on top of a circle. Now look for that in the answers. Can you find it?

Inspiration :
Mimmo Castellano - Artist style

Answers :
Second box starting from the left

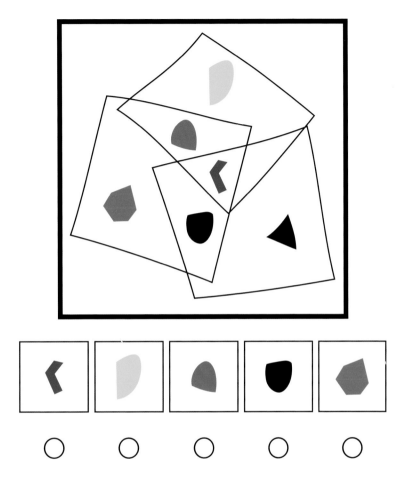

Three Questions:

1. Point to the shape that is yellow but only inside one other shape.
2. Now which shape is inside three other shapes? (Point to that shape).
3. Which shape is inside two other shapes and is not black?

Hints :

Take these steps one by one. First, draw the star and the diamond switching. Now draw the circle moving under the new diamond's spot. Now look for the drawing at the bottom which looks like that.

Inspiration :
Yayoi Kusama - Flowers that
bloom at midnight

Answers :
Second box starting from the left

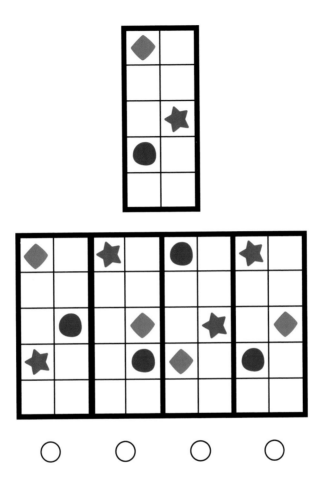

Read out loud one time.

At the top we have a circle a star and a diamond. If the star and the diamond switched spots, and the circle moved under the new diamond's spot, which drawing would it look like?

Hints :

Does it ever rain cats and dogs? Does "it's raining cats and dogs" sound like a lot of rain or no rain? So which picture shows what the weather probably is?

Inspiration :
Jared chapman- Drawing of a dog

Answers :
Second box starting from the left

"What's the weather like" asked Mike.
"It's raining cats and dogs," said his mom.
Point to the picture that shows the weather outside.

Letter Recognition and Phonemic Awareness

Letter Recognition and Phonemic Awareness are skills that are foundational to students' early literacy. While they are not on many gifted and talented tests, they are often tested by private schools — whether through the AABL test, the Kindergarten Readiness Test, or through individual school assessments.

Letter recognition begins with whether or not children know the sounds and shape of each letter. To test this, students are asked to point to letters when they are told their name or sound, and students are further asked to figure out the letter that words start with based on their sound. For instance, a student might be asked, "what letter does the word "bear" begin with?" or to point to the letter that makes an "s" sound as in "snake." This is pretty self-explanatory to most parents. Because this is substantive knowledge (the alphabet), we have not given lots of practice on these types of questions. There are of course many, many resources out there to help your child learn the alphabet.

Phonemic awareness questions look at the individual sounds involved in words. Questions might ask students which words rhyme and which do not, or which group of words begin with the same letter. Other questions might ask students to find words that have the same number of syllables as other words. Phonemic awareness questions test the ability of student to make sense of the differences in how words sound. This is a knowledge that develops over use and practice with language, and the best way to help students learn this knowledge is of course simply to read with them stories and poems that they enjoy. Rhyming books are especially helpful to practice phonemic awareness, and simply rhyming words while you talk with them is a simple and fun way to practice the skill. Let them search for rhymes to simple words to continue the pattern. Don't even worry if they aren't real words — children love making up silly rhymes and usually delight in ones that aren't even real.

Hints :
Try writing out the alphabet by singing the song.
Now look for each letter asked for in the question.

Answers :
1) Third box starting from the left on the third row
2) First box starting from the left on the third row
3) Fourth box starting from the left on the first row
4) Second box starting from the left on the second row

Inspiration :
Giambattista Bodoni -
Bodoni typeface sketch

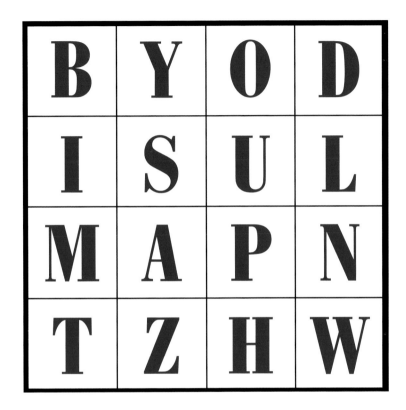

Point to the letter P. Point to the letter M. Point to the letter that makes the "D" sound as in dog. Point to the letter than makes the "S" sound as in snake.

Hints :

Try saying each picture out loud. Did any of the words rhyme? Say all the pictures again. Do any of the words rhyme with snake? Do any of the words rhyme with frog?

Inspiration :

Marjane Satrapi - Artist style

Answers :

1) The first and second box starting from the left

2) The first and second box starting from the left

3) The first and second box starting from the left

4) D: Dog, first box starting from the left on the first row,

R: Rake, second box starting from the left on the second row

1. On the first row, point to the two that rhyme?
2. On the second row, point to the two that rhyme.
3. On the third row, point to the two that rhyme.
4. Look at the whole picture - which of these start with the letter "D as in Day?"
What about the letter "R" as in Red?

Hints :

Let's start by saying the names of each animal.

What sound does cow start with? What about cat? What about ram? Does ram sound different?

Words with one syllable are short - dog, cat, cow. Words with two syllables are a bit longer. All of these words have two syllables - kitty, birdy, cookie, lady.

Do any of the animals in the picture have words that are two syllables?

Answers :

1) First row : Third box starting from the left

Second row : Fourth box starting from the left

Third row: Fourth box starting from the left

2) Lobster(Third box second row),

Eagle(Fourth box second row),

Lion(First box second row)

3) Ladybug (Second box second row),

Elephant (Fourth box third row),

Butterfly(Third box third row)

Inspiration :
Mimmo Castellano -
Il purosangue cover

1. Point to the animal in each row that doesn't start with the same letters as the other words in that row.
2. The word "Tiger" has two syllables. Ti-ger. Point to the animals above that have two syllables.
3. The word "Flamingo" has 3 syllables. Fla-ming-go. Point to the animals above that have 3 syllables.

Number Recognition and Geometric Fluency

Number Recognition and Geometric Fluency questions test whether students have learned to recognize the symbols that make up our number and shape systems. As with literacy, this more substantive knowledge is usually not tested by Gifted and Talented tests, but is often tested by private schools, whether on the AABL, the KRT, or on individual private school assessments.

Usually, students are expected to be familiar with the numerals from zero to twenty (0 to 20), and so we have asked them a smattering of those numbers here. Students are expected to be able to name each of these numbers based on the numeral, and to order the numerals from smallest to largest. It should be noted that students are usually expected to understand early arithmetic as well — the addition and subtraction of small numbers. However, this is usually tested with objects not numerals and thus is covered (in this book) in quantitative reasoning.

Similarly, students are expected to be familiar with the names of common shapes and how we speak about them. Triangles, squares, rectangles, circles, stars, crescents, and potentially other shapes are asked of them, and students are asked to determine their relative sizes and dimensions — the largest or smallest shapes, the skinniest or fattest shapes, the tallest or shortest shapes and so on. Along these same lines, students are often asked to understand the concept of measurement in its simplest forms — from the measurement of length to the measurement of heat or the measurement of time.

Engaging young children in all of the measurement that happens in our daily life — from how hot the oven is to how tall they have become — is the simplest and likely most engaging way to give them practice with the concepts of measurements. There are many ways to introduce shapes to young students as well — from drawing shapes, to building shapes with blocks, to playing "I spy" a shape as you take a walk with them.

As for learning their numerals, as with anything, it's wise to have a physical number set they can hold, feel and see along with any numerals they encounter on the page or screen. There are many simple games you can play to teach young students their numerals. Most young children enjoy counting and will happily engage in placing numerals on the right number of objects as a simple game: "How many toy race-cars do you have? Seven? Okay, let's place the number seven next to the race-cars... How many stuffed animals?"

Hints :

Try writing all the numbers in order from 1 to 20. Now look for the numbers five, nine and eighteen. Find them in the puzzle.

Inspiration :
Albrecht Dürer -
Fraktur script sketches

Answers :
1) Fourth box starting from the left on the first row
2) Second box starting from the left on the first row
3) Second box starting from the left on the third row
4) Fourth box starting from the left on the fourth row
5) First box starting from the left on the first row

1	9	17	5
12	3	0	8
10	7	2	13
6	18	4	20

Point to the number five. Point to the number nine. Point to the number eighteen. Point to the largest number. Point to the smallest number.

Hints :

Which shapes do you know the names of?
Which ones don't you know the names of?
Triangles have three corners - how many corners does the square have?

Answers :
1) Second box starting form the left on the second row
2) Third box starting form the left on the second row
3) Fourth box starting form the left on the third row
4) Third box starting form the left on the first row
5) Four corners :First box starting form the left on the
second row and the third box starting from
the left on the third row

Inspiration :
Daniel Entonado - Collage

Circle the smallest. Circle the tallest. Circle the widest. Circle the triangle. Circle the shapes that have four corners.

Acknowledgements

The puzzles here are for kids, but such great puzzles lay before us as parents. How do we chart a course to protect our children from the thousand traps set by modern capitalism - from the omni-peddling of sugar and junk food to the allure of endless tv on demand? How do we let our kids develop freely in the endless world of their imaginations and still help them navigate an educational system which each year pushes to further break down the life of the mind into additional rote tasks, graded according to mechanical precision? How do wind our way through this thicket? I have a secret weapon: my partner, Susana. Susie, this book is dedicated to you, whose clarity, insight and love is endlessly inspiring. And it is dedicated to Lucas, our four year old son, our fearless leader, racing us down the pathways of the imagination, who has shown, without a doubt, that deep in that forest playground, everything somehow works itself out.